Good Housekeeping Cookery Club

EBURY PRESS
LONDON

First published 1995

1 3 5 7 9 10 8 6 4 2

First published in the United Kingdom in 1995 by Ebury Press,
Random House, 20 Vauxhall Bridge Road, London SW1V 2SA

Random House Australia (Pty) Limited
20 Alfred Street, Milsons Point, Sydney,
New South Wales 2061, Australia

Random House New Zealand Limited
18 Poland Road, Glenfield,
Auckland 10, New Zealand

Random House South Africa (Pty) Limited
PO Box 337, Bergvlei, South Africa

Random House UK Limited Reg. No. 954009

A CIP catalogue record for this book is available from the
British Library.

Managing Editor: JANET ILLSLEY
Design: SARA KIDD
Special Photography: LAURIE EVANS
Food Stylist: LOUISE PICKFORD
Photographic Stylist: LESLEY RICHARDSON
Techniques Photography: KARL ADAMSON
Food Techniques Stylist: ANGELA KINGSBURY
Recipes created by: THE NATIONAL MAGAZINE COMPANY LTD and
CLARE GORDON-SMITH
Recipe Testing: EMMA-LEE GOW

ISBN 0 09 179099 9

Typeset in Gill Sans by Textype Typesetters, Cambridge
Colour Separations by Magnacraft, London
Printed and bound in Italy by New Interlitho Italia S.p.a., Milan

CONTENTS

COOKERY NOTES

- Both metric and imperial measures are given for the recipes. Follow either metric or imperial throughout as they are not interchangeable.
- All spoon measures are level unless otherwise stated. Sets of measuring spoons are available in both metric and imperial for accurate measurements of small quantities.
- Ovens should be preheated to the specified temperature. Grills should also be preheated. The cooking times given in the recipes assume that this has been done.
- Where a stage is specified in brackets under freezing instructions, the dish should be frozen at the end of that stage.
- Size 2 eggs should be used except where otherwise specified. Free-range eggs are recommended.
- Use freshly ground black pepper and sea salt unless otherwise specified.
- Use fresh rather than dried herbs unless dried herbs are suggested in the recipe.
- Stocks should be freshly made if possible. Alternatively buy ready-made stocks or use good quality stock cubes.

INTRODUCTION

A healthy diet is an important component of a healthy lifestyle – a lifestyle which can help ensure that we remain fit and healthy in later life. There is no longer any doubt that the food we eat can have an important effect on our health and well-being. Conditions such as coronary heart disease, strokes, hypertension, arthritis and obesity are all known to be linked to our diet. 30% of all cancers are believed to be diet-related.

In Mediterranean countries, such as Greece and southern Italy, where most people eat more fruit and vegetables, less fat and more starchy carbohydrate foods than we do, the incidence of diet related diseases is far less common.

In the United Kingdom we are in the unenviable position of being at the top of an international league table for deaths from coronary heart disease. One in five men and one in seven women under the age of 65 die prematurely as a result of coronary heart disease. Hundreds of studies from around the world have shown that it makes sense to choose a healthy diet.

Healthy eating doesn't mean that you're condemned to a life of eating lettuce leaves, lentils and cottage cheese – and it doesn't mean that you have to give up the foods you enjoy. There are no such things as 'good' and 'bad' or 'healthy' and 'unhealthy' foods – it's your diet in it's entirety that's important. The occasional ice cream, chocolate bar or cream cake certainly won't do any harm.

In the last 5 years two comprehensive nutritional reports on healthy eating have produced guidelines for a healthy diet which suggest that most people in this country should:

- Aim to eat at least five portions of fruit and vegetables (not including potatoes) a day.
- Reduce total fat intake so that it provides no more than 30% of our total calories.
- Increase fibre intake to an average of 18g (⅔ oz) fibre a day.
- Aim to obtain almost half our daily calories from complex carbohydrates found in starchy foods such as bread, potatoes, rice, pasta and breakfast cereals.

But what does all this mean in terms of the food we eat? It simply means that we need to eat more of some foods such as fruit and vegetables, and rather less of others such as those which contain large amounts of fat and sugar.

Eating a wide variety of foods is important to ensure that your diet provides all the nutrients necessary for good health. Foods can be divided into five main groups. You need to eat some food from each group every day, but the key to a healthy diet is to get the balance right. The food groups are as follows:

FRUIT AND VEGETABLES

Basically the more fruit and vegetables you eat the better. Most people in this country need to double the amount they already eat in order to reach the recommended intake. Fruit and vegetables are low in fat and calories (with the notable exceptions of avocados and olives). They also contain useful amounts of dietary fibre, particularly soluble fibre – a good intake of which can help reduce high blood cholesterol levels.

Most fruit and vegetables provide valuable amounts of vitamin C, the richest sources being citrus fruits, kiwi fruit, strawberries and peppers. The highly coloured fruit and vegetables, such as apricots, pumpkin, spinach, red peppers and carrots, are a good source of beta-carotene, which the body converts into vitamin A.

Beta-carotene and vitamin C are known as antioxidant vitamins. A good intake of these will help protect the body from the damaging effects of free radicals – highly reactive molecules which are believed to be involved in the initiation of conditions such as cancer, coronary heart disease, cataracts and arthritis.

The following suggestions may help you to get into the habit of eating more fruit and vegetables. Aim for a minimum of five servings a day; one serving is equivalent to approximately half a cup of cooked vegetables or one piece of fruit.

- Try to make sure that you eat some fruit and vegetables at each meal.
- Eat fruit as a snack in between meals.
- Keep the fruit bowl full and on display to jog your memory.
- Add a chopped banana or some dried apricots to your breakfast cereal. When they're in season add some soft fruits, such as raspberries or strawberries.
- Include extra vegetables in savoury dishes like macaroni cheese and lasagne.
- Make your own vegetable soups – they are inexpensive, quick and easy, and far superior in flavour to the canned alternatives.
- Keep some frozen vegetables in the freezer – they are economical, require little in the way of preparation and you can take out just the amount you need.
- Be adventurous – most supermarkets and greengrocers now stock a good variety of fruit and vegetables – don't choose the same ones week after week.
- Aim to eat a vegetable-based meal, such as ratatouille, a pasta dish or stir-fried vegetables, at least once a week.
- Buy what's in season – not only will it be cheaper, it will also taste better.
- If you're concerned about pesticide residues buy organic produce, which is now available from many supermarkets.

BREAD, GRAINS, RICE, BREAKFAST CEREALS, PASTA, POTATOES

Foods from this group provide fibre, protein, vitamins, particularly those from the B group, and minerals such as calcium and iron. These are the foods to fill up on – they should provide the bulk of our calories. To meet the current healthy eating targets most people need to double their present intake.

In the past these foods were believed to be fattening and many people still avoid them for this reason, which is a mistake. They're low in fat and because they contain appreciable amounts

A healthy diet will include a wide range of fresh fruit and vegetables. Make the most of fresh produce when it is in season, and at its best. These fruits and vegetables are good sources of vitamin C and fibre. Carrots are an excellent source of beta-carotene, which is converted to vitamin A in the body.

of fibre they help satisfy the appetite. However, it is worth noting that when eaten in combination with fat – when deep-fried for example – they become extremely calorific: 125 g (4 oz) boiled potatoes contains 80 calories, compared with the same weight of chipped potatoes which contains 250 calories!

Wholemeal bread is made from the wholegrain and therefore contains more fibre and B vitamins than refined white bread, but eating plenty of bread of any kind is good for you. Really fresh bread has the added advantage that it doesn't need butter or any other spread – so if possible buy little and often.

Breakfast cereals are usually low in fat and a good source of vitamins and minerals. Wholegrain cereals provide insoluble fibre, a good intake of which helps keep the digestive system working efficiently. Porridge oats and oat-based cereals provide soluble fibre which can help to reduce high blood cholesterol levels.

Wholemeal flour contains more fibre and B vitamins than white; some recipes work well with wholemeal flour, others don't. If you would like to use wholemeal flour but find it a little too heavy, start by using half wholemeal and half white, then gradually increase the proportion of wholemeal. As with wholemeal flour, many people find wholemeal pasta and brown rice just a little too heavy. There is absolutely no need to sacrifice good taste in the name of a healthy diet – it's easy enough to increase your fibre intake in other ways.

MILK AND DAIRY PRODUCTS (CHEESE, YOGURT, FROMAGE FRAIS)

Foods from this group are a major source of calcium – which is essential for strong bones. They also provide protein, vitamins A, D, B1, B6, B2, B12 and folic acid. Most dairy products also contain large amounts of fat, most of which is saturated, and for this reason they should only be eaten in moderation. Using reduced-fat varieties such as skimmed and semi-skimmed milk can help control fat intake. Sauces and custards made with skimmed milk will taste hardly any different to those made with full cream milk.

FISH, MEAT, POULTRY, EGGS, NUTS AND PULSES

Foods from this group provide protein, fat, vitamins and minerals. Fish is quick to cook, versatile and extremely nutritious. White fish, such as cod and haddock, contain very little fat. Look out for some of the more unusual varieties such as huss, hake and pollock which can be used as an alternative to cod. Oily fish, such as salmon, mackerel and herring, contain more fat but it is the polyunsaturated type, rich in omega 3 fatty acids, which nutritionists believe may be helpful in preventing heart disease and treating conditions such as psoriasis and arthritis. Fish is an excellent source of protein and vitamins A and D.

Recent studies have shown that people who eat fish two or three times a week have a significantly lower rate of heart disease. Canned fish, such as tuna and sardines, are good storecupboard ingredients – they are convenient, economical and nutritious. If you are counting calories, choose fish canned in brine or tomato sauce rather than fish in oil.

Shellfish are sometimes criticised for being high in cholesterol, but they contain very little fat. The level of cholesterol in our blood is influenced much more by the amount and type of fat in our diet than by the amount of cholesterol we consume.

Meat – and red meat in particular – has received a great deal of bad press in recent years. Many people have become vegetarian in the belief that it will automatically make their diet healthier, but this isn't necessarily the case. Although a vegetarian diet can be a very healthy way of eating – low in saturated fat, high in fibre and nutritionally complete – it is important to ensure that you replace the nutrients that you would normally get from meat, particularly iron and vitamin B12.

Chicken can play a valuable role in a calorie-conscious diet as it is low in fat and high in protein and vitamins.

A healthy diet needn't exclude

red meat, but it certainly isn't necessary to eat meat every day. Choose lean cuts of meat and trim away any visible fat before cooking. Use smaller quantities of meat in stews and casseroles and bulk them out with plenty of vegetables or by adding beans.

Eggs provide protein, vitamin A, vitamin B1, B2, B12 and folic acid. Egg yolks contain a high level of cholesterol, but it is the amount and type of fat in the diet rather than the level of cholesterol in individual foods which will affect blood cholesterol levels. Because of the risk of salmonella poisoning the Department of Health recommends that dishes containing raw or lightly cooked eggs should be avoided by 'at-risk groups', particularly young children, the elderly, pregnant women and anyone with an immune deficiency disease.

Beans and pulses are naturally low in fat and an excellent source of protein, soluble fibre and vitamins, particularly those from the B group. All dried beans (with the exception of lentils and split peas) should be soaked overnight in plenty of cold water. The next day drain, rinse and place in a saucepan with fresh cold water. Bring to the boil and boil rapidly for 10 minutes to destroy toxins which are naturally present in some types of bean, then simmer until tender. Salt should not be added until towards the end of the cooking time otherwise it will cause the skins to toughen.

As an alternative to soaking the beans overnight, put them in a saucepan, cover with cold water and bring to the boil. Boil rapidly for 10 minutes, then remove from the heat, cover the pan and leave the beans to soak in the same water for 3 hours. Drain, rinse and cook in fresh water until tender. Dried beans can be cooked in bulk and then frozen until required. Canned beans are a good alternative.

FATS, OILS AND SUGARY FOODS

Small amounts of fat are necessary in our diet to provide essential fatty acids and to allow the absorption of the fat-soluble vitamins A, D, K and E. Fat also helps to make our food palatable, giving it texture and flavour. However, the majority of people in this country eat far too much fat. Healthy eating recommendations suggest that fat should account for no more than 30% of our total energy intake.

For good health we should aim for a balance between the three different types of fat – saturated, mono-unsaturated and polyunsaturated. Olive oil, peanuts and peanut oil, avocado pears and rape seed oil all contain high levels of mono-unsaturated fats. Vegetable and seed oils, oily fish and lean meat provide mainly polyunsaturated fatty acids. Use oils rich in mono- and polyunsaturated fatty acids to make salad dressings and for sautéeing and stir-frying.

Saturated fatty acids are found predominantly in animal fats such as the fat in meat and dairy products. Diets which contain high levels of saturated fat are known to increase the risks of heart disease and certain types of cancer. However this doesn't mean that these foods need to be avoided completely – simply that they should be eaten in moderation. Whatever type of fat you choose to use for cooking and spreading onto bread the most important thing to remember is to use it sparingly!

Like fat, sugar helps to make food palatable and – like fat – most of us eat more than is recommended for good health. Sugar provides calories but nothing else in the way of protein, fibre, vitamins or minerals. Most people in this country consume far more calories than their bodies actually need. This is reflected in the number of obese people in the UK: 32% of men and 36% of women. Obesity is not merely a cosmetic problem – it is known to increase the risk of a number of illnesses.

Contrary to popular belief, brown sugar and honey have no nutritional advantage over white sugar although some people prefer the taste. Like fat it is really not necessary to avoid sugar completely but it makes good sense to think about the amount that we eat: sugar provides 'empty calories' – calories which most people could well do without.

COOKING FOR HEALTH

A healthy diet isn't simply determined by the foods we eat. The way in which these foods are prepared and cooked can have a significant effect on their nutritional values. The vitamins in fruit and vegetables, in particular, are easily destroyed during storage, preparation and cooking. To ensure freshness, buy little and often, from a shop with a quick turnover, and store vegetables in a cool dark place, ideally for no more than 3 days. Always eat food as soon as you can after it is cooked; keeping food warm results in some vitamin loss. Remember that some cooking methods are healthier than others, too. Frying food in a large amount of fat will obviously add on calories in the form of saturated fats. The cooking methods described below are beneficial for a healthy eating pattern.

GRILLING

Grilling is an excellent way of cooking meat, fish, poultry and some vegetables. It requires little or no fat to be added during cooking and is therefore a much healthier alternative to frying. Grilling is ideal for cooking tender, even-sized cuts of meat which are not too thick. It's not suitable for tough cuts of meat as the intense heat will toughen the texture of the fibres even more. Marinating food before grilling will improve the flavour and help tenderise meat. Leave the food in the marinade for at least 1 hour, preferably overnight. Grilling is a good method for cooking oily fish such as mackerel and herrings. Care must be taken when grilling delicate white fish, as they can dry out quickly. Vegetables, such as mushrooms, courgettes, peppers, aubergines and tomatoes, can be grilled successfully. They should be brushed with oil first and cooked under a moderate heat.

STIR-FRYING

Stir-fried food has a good texture and flavour. It's a quick method of cooking and this helps to preserve vitamins as well as the flavour. Much less fat is required than for shallow-frying. Make sure that all the vegetables are cut into pieces of the same size so that they cook in the same amount of time. Use a wok or deep-sided frying pan and ensure that the oil is really hot before adding the ingredients.

ROASTING

This is a healthy way of cooking meat and poultry. Place the joint or bird on a rack over a roasting tin so that the fat drips underneath. Remove any fat before using the remaining juices to make gravy. Roasting is an excellent way of cooking certain vegetables such as aubergines, courgettes, onions, garlic and peppers. Cut the vegetables into large chunks, blanch in boiling water and thoroughly drain. Place in a large roasting tin, drizzle with olive oil, season well and cook in a moderate oven until tender.

STEAMING

Steaming is one of the best methods for cooking vegetables. It helps to retain their flavour, colour and most importantly the water-soluble vitamins which are easily lost during other cooking methods, particularly boiling. Special steamers are available in which water is boiled in the bottom compartment and the food is cooked in a compartment above. Alternatively you can use a metal basket-type steamer which will fit into a saucepan. They are available from most cookware shops, are easy to use and inexpensive to buy. Other foods such as fish and grains can also be steamed.

MICROWAVE COOKING

Microwaves cook food very quickly and without the need to add extra fat or large amounts of water. This method therefore helps to retain vitamins, particularly the water-soluble B vitamins and vitamin C, that can easily be destroyed by other cooking methods. It is particularly useful for cooking vegetables and fish, and for defrosting and reheating food quickly.

BOILING

The water-soluble vitamins present in vegetables can very easily be lost during this method of cooking. Boiling vegetables in large quantities of water can destroy up to 70% of their vitamin C content.

To help preserve the vitamins, add the vegetables to a small amount of boiling water and cook for as short a time as possible, until they are just tender but retain some 'bite'. To retain some of the water-soluble vitamins which dissolve in the liquid, use the vegetable water to make gravy, stock or soup.

STEWING

This long, slow cooking method is ideal for tenderising tougher cuts of meat. The meat is cooked with vegetables and flavourings in just enough liquid to cover them. If they are made the day before they are needed, stews and casseroles can be quickly cooled, refrigerated, and then any excess fat can be removed from the surface easily before they are reheated.

FRESH COURGETTE AND PEA SOUP

A light refreshing soup which is ideal to serve in the height of the summer when fresh peas are in season. The combination of peas with courgettes and leeks makes a pretty soup with plenty of flavour. For a really fresh-tasting soup, make your own pesto (see below). When fresh peas are not available, use frozen ones instead.

SERVES 4-6

2 leeks
450 g (1 lb) fresh peas (in the pod)
2 small courgettes
15 ml (1 tbsp) olive oil
600 ml (1 pint) chicken or vegetable stock
salt and pepper
30-45 ml (2-3 tbsp) pesto sauce

PREPARATION TIME
20 minutes
COOKING TIME
15-20 minutes
FREEZING
Suitable

170-110 CALS PER SERVING

1. Prepare the vegetables. Trim the leeks and wash thoroughly, then slice into rounds. Remove the peas from their pods. Chop or grate the courgettes.

2. Heat the olive oil in a large saucepan, add the vegetables and sauté gently for a few minutes. Heat the stock, then pour onto the vegetables and bring to the boil. Lower the heat, cover and simmer for about 15 minutes until the vegetables are just tender, but still retaining their colour. Check the seasoning.

3. Pour the soup into warmed bowls, swirl in the pesto and serve at once. Toasted French bread makes an ideal accompaniment.

VARIATION

Use 225 g (8 oz) frozen peas in place of the fresh ones. Replace the courgette with the heart of a soft lettuce.

PESTO SAUCE: To make your own version, simply put 1 peeled garlic clove, 5 ml (1 tsp) sea salt, 50 g (2 oz) pine nuts, 3 large handfuls of fresh basil leaves, 90 ml (3 fl oz) olive oil and 15 ml (1 tbsp) freshly grated Parmesan cheese in a blender or food processor and work until smooth.

TECHNIQUE

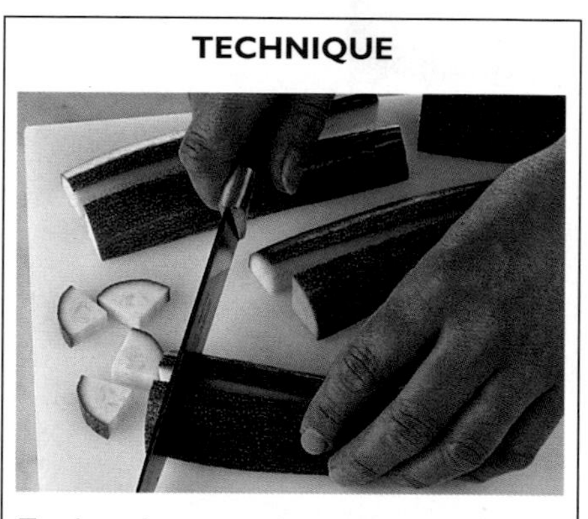

To chop the courgettes, quarter each one lengthwise, then slice crosswise.

SPICY PARSNIP AND CARROT SOUP WITH CUMIN

A wonderfully warming vegetarian soup, with a delicious hint of spicy cumin seeds. As the parsnip and carrot purée is sufficient to thicken the soup, there are no added calories in the form of flour – making it an ideal recipe for slimmers. For optimum flavour, use homemade vegetable stock. Serve the soup as a sustaining lunch, accompanied by wholemeal bread or crusty rolls.

SERVES 4

1 onion
450 g (1 lb) parsnips
225 g (8 oz) carrots
30 ml (2 tbsp) olive oil
15 ml (1 tbsp) curry powder
350 ml (¾ pint) vegetable stock
300 ml (½ pint) semi-skimmed milk
salt and pepper
TO GARNISH
10 ml (2 tsp) cumin seeds

PREPARATION TIME
15 minutes
COOKING TIME
15-20 minutes
FREEZING
Suitable

200 CALS PER SERVING

1. Peel and finely chop the onion. Peel the parsnips, cut in half and remove the woody stems. Peel the carrots. Cut the parsnips and carrots into even-sized pieces.

2. Heat the olive oil in a heavy-based saucepan, add the vegetables and stir to lightly coat in the oil. Cover and cook for a few minutes until the vegetables are slightly softened. Sprinkle in the curry powder and cook, stirring, for 1 minute.

3. Stir in the vegetable stock and milk, and season with salt and pepper. Bring to the boil, then reduce the heat to a gentle simmer and cook for 15-20 minutes until the vegetables are soft.

4. Allow the soup to cool a little, then transfer to a blender or food processor and work until smooth. If the consistency is a little too thick for your liking, add a dash more milk or vegetable stock.

5. Toast the cumin seeds by gently frying them in a non-stick pan, or spread on a baking sheet and grill under a medium heat. Meanwhile, return the soup to the saucepan and reheat gently. Serve the soup in warmed soup bowls, garnished with a sprinkling of cumin seeds.

VARIATIONS

Use pumpkin in place of carrots for a vibrant soup with an excellent flavour. Alternatively, use a mixture of root vegetables, such as swede, parsnip and potato.

TECHNIQUE

Purée the soup in a blender or food processor, then return to the saucepan and reheat gently.

SEAFOOD SOUP WITH LOW-FAT ROUILLE

It's worth making your own stock for this traditional soup, to obtain a true rich seafood flavour. Buy fresh cooked prawns, peel them yourself and use the shells as the basis for the enriched stock. Adding a few shelled scallops to the soup will further enhance the flavour.

SERVES 4

450 g (1 lb) cooked prawns in shell
600 ml (1 pint) fish stock
150 ml (1/4 pint) dry white wine
2 fresh parsley sprigs
2 bay leaves
4 fresh tarragon sprigs
2 onions, peeled
15 g (½ oz) butter
15 g (½ oz) flour
300 ml (½ pint) semi-skimmed milk
salt and pepper
ROUILLE
1 small red chilli
1 garlic clove
60 ml (4 tbsp) low-fat mayonnaise
30 ml (2 tbsp) low-fat fromage frais
cayenne pepper
TO SERVE
8 slices of French bread

PREPARATION TIME
20 minutes
COOKING TIME
35-40 minutes
FREEZING
Not suitable

200 CALS PER SERVING

1. Shell the prawns and set aside. Put the prawn shells in a saucepan with the fish stock, wine, parsley, bay leaves, tarragon and one of the onions, halved. Bring to the boil, lower the heat, cover and simmer for 20 minutes. Strain the stock through a fine sieve into a jug.

2. Finely chop the remaining onion. Heat the butter in a large saucepan, stir in the onion and sauté gently until softened. Add the flour and cook, stirring, for 1-2 minutes.

3. Gradually pour in the fish stock, stirring constantly, then add the milk. Bring to the boil, stirring, then add the prawns. Simmer gently for 15-20 minutes. Allow to cool slightly, then transfer to a blender or food processor and work until smooth.

4. Meanwhile make the rouille. Halve the chilli, remove the seeds, then chop the flesh very finely. Peel and crush the garlic and mix into the mayonnaise, then stir in the fromage frais, chilli and cayenne pepper to taste. Alternatively, place the ingredients in a food processor and work until smooth.

5. To serve, return the soup to the saucepan and reheat gently. Check the seasoning. Toast the French bread slices on both sides and top with the rouille. Divide the soup between warmed serving bowls and float 2 slices of rouille-topped toast on each portion. Serve at once, sprinkled with cayenne and coarsely ground pepper.

TECHNIQUE

Carefully peel the prawns, placing the shells in a saucepan for the enriched stock.

COUSCOUS-FILLED AUBERGINES WITH A CORIANDER DRESSING

Small aubergines are perfect ready-made containers for tasty fillings. Here they are stuffed with a delicious mixture of couscous, sun-dried tomatoes, dried apricots and pine nuts. Serve either hot or cold, as a starter or light meal. A tomato salad makes an ideal accompaniment.

SERVES 4

2 small aubergines, each about 250 g (9 oz)
30 ml (2 tbsp) lemon juice
sea salt and pepper
50 g (2 oz) couscous
6 sun-dried tomatoes in oil
25 g (1 oz) dried apricots (no-need-to-soak)
8 fresh mint sprigs
15 ml (1 tbsp) pine nuts
4 spring onions, trimmed

CORIANDER DRESSING

1 cm (½ inch) piece fresh root ginger
1 garlic clove, peeled
150 ml (¼ pint) low-fat bio yogurt
finely grated rind of 1 lime
30 ml (2 tbsp) chopped fresh coriander
squeeze of lime juice

TO GARNISH

coriander sprigs

PREPARATION TIME
30 minutes
COOKING TIME
20-30 minutes, plus reheating
FREEZING Not suitable

160 CALS PER SERVING

1. Preheat the oven to 200°C (400°F) Mark 6. Cut the aubergines in half lengthways and score the cut sides deeply, without damaging the skins. Place, scored-side up, on a baking sheet. Rub in the lemon juice and sprinkle with a little sea salt. Bake in the oven for 20-30 minutes until the flesh is soft and tender.

2. Meanwhile, put the couscous in a bowl and pour on 150 ml (¼ pint) boiling water. Leave to soak and fluff up while preparing the rest of the filling.

3. Drain and chop the sun-dried tomatoes; chop the dried apricots, mint, pine nuts and spring onions. Mix together in a bowl, seasoning with salt and pepper.

4. Scoop the flesh out from the cooked aubergines and chop finely. Fork through the soaked couscous to separate the grains, then add the chopped aubergine and sun-dried tomato mixture. Stir gently, using a fork, until evenly combined.

5. Spoon the filling into the aubergine shells, piling it up well. If serving hot, return to the oven for 15 minutes to heat through. Alternatively allow to cool, then chill in the refrigerator.

6. To make the dressing, peel and finely grate the ginger; crush the garlic. In a bowl, mix the yogurt with the ginger, garlic, lime rind, coriander and lime juice to taste. Chill until ready to serve.

7. Serve the filled aubergines hot or cold, garnished with coriander and topped with a generous dollop of the coriander dressing.

VARIATION

Other vegetables can be used instead of – or as well as – aubergines. Try baby peppers, baby courgettes and tomatoes.

TECHNIQUE

Carefully scoop the cooked flesh from the aubergine halves, without damaging the skins.

ROASTED VEGETABLES IN GARLIC BREAD BASKETS

Wholemeal bread baskets are rubbed with garlic, baked until crisp, then filled with a selection of roasted Mediterranean vegetables to delicious effect. Drizzling the baskets with a little balsamic vinegar lifts the flavour and a pretty garnish of basil and black olive slivers adds the finishing touch. An attractive starter to complement any meal.

SERVES 6

2 red onions
2 garlic cloves, peeled
1 yellow pepper
1 red pepper
1 small aubergine
2 courgettes
15 ml (1 tbsp) olive oil
pinch of sea salt
4 fresh rosemary sprigs
12 slices wholemeal bread
15 ml (1 tbsp) black olive paste
15 ml (1 tbsp) balsamic vinegar
TO GARNISH
12 basil sprigs
few black olives, stoned and sliced

PREPARATION TIME
30 minutes
COOKING TIME
20-30 minutes
FREEZING
Not suitable

215 CALS PER SERVING

1. Preheat the oven to 230°C (450°F) Mark 8. Peel the onions and slice lengthwise. Halve one of the garlic cloves and set aside; crush the other garlic clove. Halve the peppers, then remove the core and seeds. Cut the peppers, aubergine and courgettes into 2.5 cm (1 inch) chunks.

2. Place all the vegetables in a roasting tin, drizzle over the olive oil and sprinkle with the sea salt, rosemary and crushed garlic. Bake in the oven for 20-30 minutes, turning occasionally until just tinged brown at the edges.

3. Remove the crusts from the bread and roll out each slice lightly. Cut a 9 cm (3½ inch) circle from each slice using a plain cutter, and rub with the halved garlic clove. Line a 12-hole deep bun tin or muffin tin with the bread rounds.

4. Place in the oven for 5 minutes. Carefully remove the bread baskets from the tin and return to the oven for 5 minutes to allow the bread to crisp.

5. Spread a little olive paste over the base of each basket. Remove the roasted vegetables from the oven and divide between the toasted bread baskets. Just before serving, drizzle a little balsamic vinegar over each basket. Garnish with sprigs of basil and slivers of black olive. Serve warm.

VARIATIONS

Use the bread baskets as containers for other combinations of vegetables, such as lightly roasted leeks, courgettes and cauliflower.

TECHNIQUE

To shape the bread baskets, line a 12-hole deep bun tin with the bread slices.

COURGETTE, TOMATO AND PESTO BAKES

This quick and easy starter is perfect for slimmers as it provides only 90 calories per portion. Chunky slices of beefsteak tomato are topped with red pesto or olive paste, courgette slices, basil and Parmesan – to resemble mini-pizzas.

SERVES 4

225 g (8 oz) courgettes
a little olive oil
2 beefsteak tomatoes, about 450 g (1 lb) total weight
30 ml (2 tbsp) red pesto sauce or olive paste
large handful of fresh basil leaves
salt and pepper
50 g (2 oz) Parmesan cheese

PREPARATION TIME
20 minutes
COOKING TIME
10 minutes
FREEZING
Not suitable

90 CALS PER SERVING

1. Preheat the oven to 200°C (400°F) Mark 6. Cut the courgettes diagonally into slices, about 5 mm (¼ inch) thick. Lightly brush a non-stick frying pan with olive oil. Cook the courgette slices in batches for about 5 minutes, turning until tender and brown on both sides. Drain on kitchen paper.

2. Cut each tomato into 3 slices, about 1 cm (½ inch) thick, and place on a lightly oiled baking sheet. Spread 5 ml (1 tsp) of pesto or olive paste on top of each tomato slice. Place 5 or 6 basil leaves in a circle on top of the pesto.

3. Arrange an overlapping circle of courgettes on the basil leaves. Season with salt and pepper.

4. Cook in the oven for 10 minutes. Transfer to warmed individual serving plates and top with thinly pared shavings of Parmesan cheese. Serve immediately, accompanied by wholemeal bread.

NOTE: The easiest way to pare fresh Parmesan cheese is using a swivel vegetable peeler. Shave the cheese from the piece directly on to each serving.

VARIATION

This recipe works equally well with mozzarella cheese: you will need about 75 g (3 oz). Assemble as above, but top each one with a thin slice of mozzarella at the end of step 3. Cook as directed, then brown under a hot grill before serving.

TECHNIQUE

Fry the courgette slices in the minimum of oil for about 5 minutes, until tender and brown on both sides.

SPICY COCONUT PRAWNS WITH FRAGRANT RICE

Prawns do have a higher fat content than some fish, but eaten in moderation they won't cause you too much harm. The oriental spice mix – of star anise, crushed garlic, coriander and fennel seeds, cloves and peppercorns, with a subtle hint of fresh ginger – makes a wonderfully tasty, spicy coating for the prawns. Served with fragrant Thai rice, flavoured with coconut and lemon, it makes a well balanced recipe, perfect for healthy entertaining. If Thai rice is unobtainable, use basmati instead.

SERVES 4

700 g (1½ lb) raw tiger prawns in shell
15 ml (1 tbsp) clear honey
50 g (2 oz) desiccated coconut
2 lemon slices
350 g (12 oz) Thai fragrant rice, or basmati rice
ORIENTAL SPICE MIX
15 ml (1 tbsp) star anise
5 ml (1 tsp) coriander seeds
5 ml (1 tsp) fennel seeds
5 ml (1 tsp) cloves
5 ml (1 tsp) black peppercorns
2.5 cm (1 inch) piece fresh root ginger
1 garlic clove, crushed
TO GARNISH
4 lemon wedges
coriander or parsley sprigs

PREPARATION TIME
35-40 minutes, plus making stock
COOKING TIME
10-15 minutes
FREEZING
Not suitable

540 CALS PER SERVING

1. First make the oriental spice mix. Place the star anise, coriander and fennel seeds, cloves and peppercorns in a spice mill and grind coarsely. Alternatively, pound together in a pestle and mortar. Peel and grate the ginger, add to the spices with the garlic and mix well. Set aside.

2. To prepare the prawns, pull away the head from the body and set aside. Using sharp kitchen scissors, snip the shell along the underside of the prawn. Pull away from the flesh, leaving the tail intact; set aside. Pull away the black intestinal thread from the centre of the prawn and discard.

3. Place the reserved shells and heads in a saucepan and add 300 ml (½ pint) water. Bring to the boil, cover and simmer for 30 minutes.

4. Meanwhile, thread the prawns onto 8 wooden kebab skewers. Brush with honey and spread with the oriental spice mix. Cover with cling film and leave to marinate for 30 minutes.

5. Meanwhile, pour 300 ml (½ pint) boiling water over the coconut and leave to infuse for 20 minutes.

6. Strain the fish stock into a large pan. Strain the coconut milk, pressing out any excess liquid from the moist coconut, and add to the pan. Add the lemon slices and bring to the boil. Rinse the rice well under running cold water, add to the boiling stock and bring back to the boil. Simmer for 10-12 minutes, until the rice is tender.

7. Meanwhile, preheat the grill to high. Cook the prawns, close to the heat, for about 5 minutes on each side, until the flesh is white and firm. Transfer to warmed serving plates and garnish with lemon wedges and coriander or parsley. Serve with the rice.

TECHNIQUE

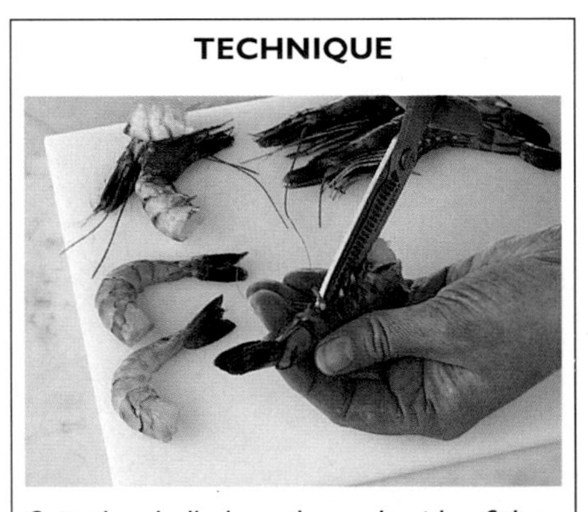

Snip the shell along the underside of the prawn. Pull away from the flesh, leaving the tail intact.

PAELLA

Paella, a traditional Spanish dish, is a typical example of the good balance of food found in the Mediterranean diet. A colourful all-in-one dish, it is excellent for an informal dinner party: easy to serve; a good combination of taste and texture; and nutritious, providing carbohydrate, protein and fibre.

SERVES 6

2 skinless chicken breast fillets
15-30 ml (1-2 tbsp) olive oil
225 g (8 oz) cleaned squid
125 g (4 oz) scallops
225 g (8 oz) mussels in shells
1 large onion
225 g (8 oz) plum tomatoes
3 garlic cloves, crushed
5 ml (1 tsp) paprika
salt and pepper
600 ml (1 pint) chicken stock
15 ml (1 tbsp) tomato purée
350 g (12 oz) risotto rice (eg Arborio)
150 ml (¼ pint) dry white wine
pinch of saffron threads
2 red peppers
125 g (4 oz) shelled peas
30 ml (2 tbsp) chopped fresh parsley

PREPARATION TIME
30 minutes
COOKING TIME
40 minutes
FREEZING
Not suitable

405 CALS PER SERVING

1. Cut each chicken breast crosswise into 4 pieces. Heat 15 ml (1 tbsp) of the oil in a paella pan, large non-stick frying pan or flameproof casserole. Toss the chicken pieces quickly in the oil to brown. Set aside.

2. Pull the ink sac from the squid and discard. Cut off the tentacles and slice the squid into thin rings. Slice each scallop into 2 or 3 rounds, depending on their thickness. Set both aside.

3. Wash the mussels thoroughly in plenty of cold water, scrubbing well, and remove the beards. Discard any which do not close when tapped firmly. Place in a large pan with about 90 ml (6 tbsp) water. Bring to the boil, then cover tightly and cook for 3-4 minutes until the shells have opened; discard any that do not open. Set aside.

4. Peel and finely chop the onion. Immerse the tomatoes in a bowl of boiling water for 1 minute. Remove from the water and pull away the skins. Chop the flesh into 1 cm (½ inch) pieces.

5. Heat the remaining oil in the same pan. Add the onion, tomatoes, garlic, paprika, salt and pepper. Stir well and cook gently for 7-10 minutes, until softened.

6. In another pan, heat the chicken stock to just below boiling point, then stir in the tomato purée.

7. Add the rice to the tomato mixture and cook, stirring, for 1 minute. Pour in 300 ml (½ pint) of the hot stock and the wine. Cook, stirring, for about 7 minutes, until the liquid has been absorbed.

8. Meanwhile, soak the saffron threads in the remaining stock. Add to the rice with the squid, scallops and chicken. Cover and simmer gently for 15 minutes.

9. Meanwhile, preheat the grill and grill the red peppers, turning, until blackened. Cover with a damp tea-towel, leave until cool enough to handle, then remove the skins. Cut the peppers in half, remove the core and seeds, then cut into thin strips.

10. Stir the peppers into the paella with the mussels, peas and parsley. Cook for a further 5 minutes. Check the seasoning and serve immediately, with a salad.

TECHNIQUE

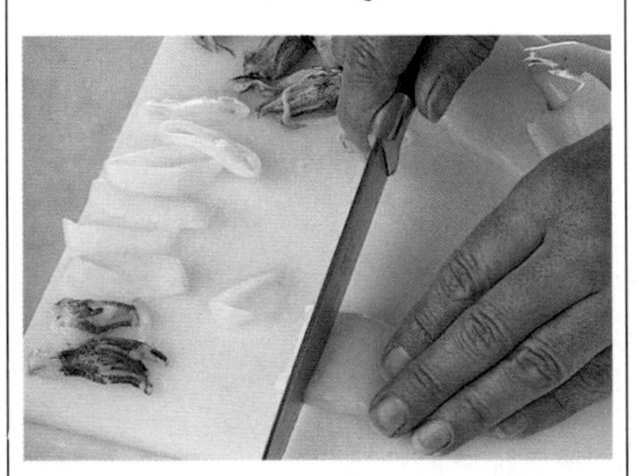

Cut off the tentacles and slice the squid into thin rings.

ROASTED MONKFISH TAILS WITH ROCKET PESTO ON A BED OF SHALLOTS

A wonderfully tender and flavoursome fish dish. Roasting the fish at a high temperature ensures it cooks quickly and is succulent. Rocket gives the pesto a good flavour as well as an intense green colour.

SERVES 4

225 g (8 oz) shallots
4 garlic cloves (unpeeled)
30 ml (2 tbsp) cider vinegar
30 ml (2 tbsp) olive oil
900 g (2 lb) monkfish tails (on the bone)
salt and pepper
4 fresh rosemary sprigs
4 fresh thyme sprigs
4 fresh oregano sprigs
ROCKET PESTO
50 g (2 oz) rocket leaves
15 g (½ oz) fresh Parmesan cheese
15 ml (1 tbsp) olive oil
30 ml (2 tbsp) apple juice

PREPARATION TIME
30 minutes
COOKING TIME
35-45 minutes
FREEZING
Not suitable

320 CALS PER SERVING

1. Preheat the oven to 220°C (425°F) Mark 7. Peel the shallots and cut in half. Place in a roasting pan with the garlic, sprinkle with the cider vinegar and oil and cook for 15-20 minutes.

2. Meanwhile, make the pesto. Wash the rocket, removing any bruised leaves. Place in a blender or food processor. Grate the Parmesan cheese and add to the blender with the oil. With the machine running, pour the apple juice through the feeder tube in a steady stream. Blend until a smooth paste is formed.

3. Remove any skin and membrane from the monkfish: cut around the membrane, pull back and tear off using your fingers.

4. Cut along one side of the centre bone, as close to the bone as possible, and remove the fillet. Repeat on the other side.

5. Lay one fillet, cut side up, on a board and spread with the pesto. Place the other fillet on top, cut side down, to sandwich the pesto. Tie the two pieces together at regular intervals with string.

6. Remove the roasting pan from the oven, push the shallots and garlic to the sides, and lay the monkfish parcel in the centre of the pan. Sprinkle with salt and pepper and add the herb sprigs. Cook for 20-25 minutes, until the monkfish turns opaque.

7. To serve, remove the string and lift the fish onto a serving platter, discarding any milky residue. Place the shallots and garlic around the fish. Serve with boiled new potatoes or simmered wild rice and steamed mangetouts.

VARIATION

Use a tail end of salmon instead of monkfish. For speed, use ready-made pesto.

TECHNIQUE

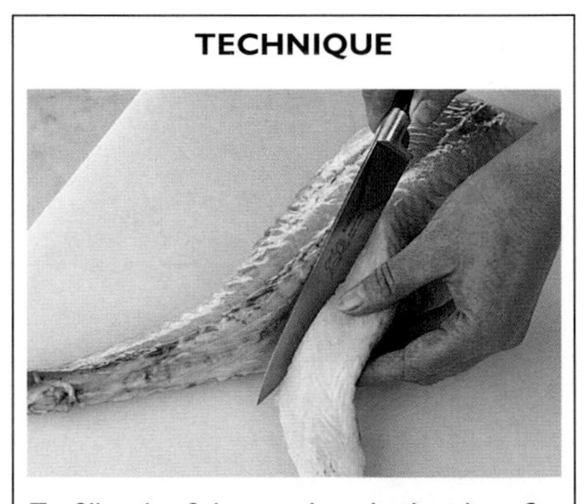

To fillet the fish, cut along both sides of the central bone, placing the knife as close as possible to the bone.

GRILLED SALMON FILLETS WITH CAPERS

These salmon fillets are sprinkled with capers and cooked on a bed of lemon and dill-flavoured leeks. The pretty pink flesh of salmon will often appeal to those who are not so keen on fish, and the wide availability of farmed salmon – now at reasonable prices – enables this 'king of fish' to be served more often.

SERVES 6

4 leeks
salt and pepper
1 lemon
15 ml (1 tbsp) snipped fresh dill
6 salmon fillets, each about 150 g (5 oz)
25 g (1 oz) capers, drained and rinsed

ORANGE AND DILL SAUCE

1 orange
15 ml (1 tbsp) low-fat mayonnaise
30 ml (2 tbsp) low-fat bio yogurt
15 ml (1 tbsp) chopped fresh dill
15 ml (1 tbsp) chopped fresh parsley

TO GARNISH

orange slices
flat-leaf parsley sprigs

PREPARATION TIME
15 minutes
COOKING TIME
About 10 minutes
FREEZING
Not suitable

310 CALS PER SERVING

1. Trim leeks, wash thoroughly and slice thinly. Blanch in a pan of boiling salted water for 2 minutes; drain.

2. Finely grate the rind from the lemon and squeeze the juice. Mix 15 ml (1 tbsp) lemon juice, the lemon rind and dill with the leeks. Lay a thin layer over the base of a shallow flameproof dish, about 20 cm (8 inches) square.

3. Skin the salmon: place a sharp knife between the flesh and skin and, with a sawing action, cut across the fish pulling the skin away.

4. Preheat the grill to high. Place the salmon on top of the leeks. Divide the capers between the fillets, pressing down well. Sprinkle with salt and pepper and drizzle over 30 ml (2 tbsp) of the lemon juice. Grill for 5-8 minutes, until the fish is just firm to the touch. (The timing will depend on the thickness of the fillets.)

5. Meanwhile, prepare the orange and dill sauce. Grate the rind from the orange and squeeze the juice. Mix the mayonnaise and yogurt together, then stir in the orange rind, juice and herbs.

6. To serve, lift the salmon fillets and leeks with a fish slice onto warmed serving plates. Garnish with orange slices and parsley, and serve with the orange and dill sauce.

VARIATION

Replace the salmon fillets with cod steaks and serve on a bed of sautéed chopped red onion.

TECHNIQUE

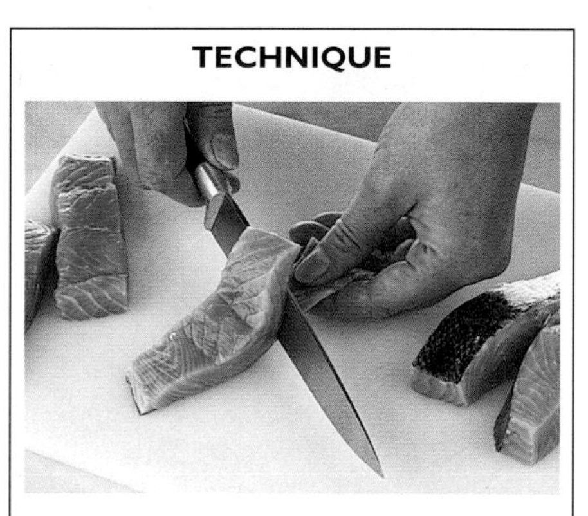

Place a sharp knife between the flesh and skin of the salmon and cut across the fish with a sawing action to remove the skin.

BAKED COD WITH HORSERADISH CRUST AND TARTARE SAUCE

These cod steaks, baked with a crumbed crust flavoured with fresh horseradish, lemon and herbs, are served with a low-fat tartare sauce. If you cannot obtain fresh horseradish, then horseradish sauce can be used as an alternative (see variation). If possible buy fresh rather than pre-packed cod. If it's very fresh, the cooked fish will have very white flakes, and an almost milky liquid will ooze out during cooking.

SERVES 6

50 g (2 oz) crustless wholemeal bread
1 lemon
30 ml (2 tbsp) chopped fresh parsley
50 g (2 oz) freshly grated horseradish
salt and pepper
6 cod steaks, each about 125 g (4 oz)
TARTARE SAUCE
6 medium gherkins
225 g (8 oz) low-fat crème fraîche
30 ml (2 tbsp) chopped fresh parsley
30 ml (2 tbsp) chopped fresh dill
TO GARNISH
lemon slices
dill sprigs

PREPARATION TIME
20 minutes
COOKING TIME
15-20 minutes
FREEZING Not suitable

210 CALS PER SERVING

1. Preheat the oven to 200°C (400°F) Mark 6. Place the bread in a food processor and process until medium to fine breadcrumbs are formed. (Alternatively, use a grater.) Place the breadcrumbs in a large bowl.

2. Grate the lemon rind and stir into the breadcrumbs with the parsley, horseradish and seasoning.

3. Place the cod steaks in a shallow roasting tin and season with salt and pepper. Divide the crust mixture between the steaks and press on firmly. Bake in the oven for 15-20 minutes, until tender.

4. Meanwhile, prepare the tartare sauce. Finely chop the gherkins and stir into the crème fraîche with the parsley and dill. Squeeze the juice from the lemon and flavour the sauce with 10-15 ml (2-3 tsp) to taste. Mix well.

5. Place the cod steaks on warmed serving plates and garnish with lemon slices and dill sprigs. Serve topped with a spoonful of the tartare sauce and accompanied by seasonal vegetables.

VARIATIONS

If fresh horseradish is unobtainable, substitute horseradish sauce. Spread 10 ml (2 tsp) over each cod steak then top with the breadcrumbs mixed with the lemon rind, parsley and seasoning. Use the crust on other mild flavoured fish, such as salmon or halibut.

TECHNIQUE

Sprinkle the fish with the breadcrumb mixture and press on firmly with the back of a spoon.

GRILLED PLAICE WITH RED PEPPER SALSA

Plaice is a good value fish to use, but often forgotten in place of more exotic species. Served like this – on a split pea purée with a red pepper salsa – it makes an unusual and tasty dish.

SERVES 4

125 g (4 oz) split yellow peas
1 onion
2 garlic cloves, crushed
1 bay leaf
6 fresh thyme sprigs
salt and pepper
30 ml (2 tbsp) plain flour
45 ml (3 tbsp) finely chopped fresh parsley
4 plaice fillets
15-30 ml (1-2 tbsp) olive oil
SALSA
1 red pepper
1 plum tomato
½ red onion
2.5 ml (½ tsp) mustard seeds
pinch of sugar
TO GARNISH
watercress sprigs

PREPARATION TIME
10 minutes
COOKING TIME
40-45 minutes
FREEZING
Not suitable

390 CALS PER SERVING

1. Rinse the split yellow peas in a sieve under running cold water, then place in a saucepan.

2. Peel and finely chop the onion and add to the split peas with the garlic, herbs and seasoning. Pour on 450 ml (¾ pint) cold water, bring to the boil, then simmer for 35-40 minutes, until soft and mushy. Drain, and remove the herb sprigs. Check the seasoning and beat to form a rough-textured purée.

3. Meanwhile, prepare the salsa. Place the pepper under a preheated hot grill and cook, turning, until blackened. Cover with a damp tea-towel and leave until cool enough to handle, then remove the skin. Cut the pepper in half and remove the core and seeds. Finely dice the pepper and place in a small bowl. Finely dice the tomato. Peel and finely chop the onion. Add the tomato and onion to the red pepper with the mustard seeds and sugar. Stir well and set aside.

4. Preheat the grill to medium. Season the flour with salt and pepper and mix in the parsley. Dip the flesh side of each plaice fillet in the mixture to coat evenly, then lay skin-side down on the grill rack. Drizzle each fillet with about 1.25 ml (¼ tsp) of the olive oil. Grill for about 5 minutes, depending on the thickness of the fillets, until the flesh turns white and is just firm to the touch.

5. To serve, place a spoonful of the split pea mixture on each warmed serving plate. Lay a fish fillet on top and spoon over 2-3 teaspoons of the salsa. Garnish with watercress.

VARIATION

Replace the plaice fillets with lemon sole fillets. Replace the grilled pepper with tomato.

TECHNIQUE

Dip the flesh side of each plaice fillet in the flour mixture to coat evenly.

RICOTTA-FILLED CHICKEN WITH TOMATO AND ORANGE SAUCE

These chicken breasts are filled with a light, fresh mixture of ricotta cheese, herbs and garlic, and served with a delicate sauce of fresh tomatoes simmered with a little orange. Serve them with a mixed leaf salad tossed in a lemon dressing – for a healthy midweek supper.

SERVES 4

175 g (6 oz) ricotta cheese
60 ml (4 tbsp) chopped fresh mixed herbs, eg oregano, thyme, parsley and chives
2 garlic cloves, crushed
salt and pepper
4 skinless chicken breast fillets, each 125-150 g (4-5 oz)
4 slices Parma ham

TOMATO AND ORANGE SAUCE
350 g (12 oz) plum tomatoes
2 shallots
1 orange
1 garlic clove, crushed
15 ml (1 tbsp) orange marmalade

TO GARNISH
orange wedges
herb sprigs

PREPARATION TIME
20 minutes
COOKING TIME
35-40 minutes
FREEZING Not suitable

315 CALS PER SERVING

1. Preheat the oven to 200°C (400°F) Mark 6. Place the ricotta cheese in a bowl and break up with a wooden spoon. Stir in the chopped herbs, garlic and seasoning.

2. Cut a 5 cm (2 inch) pocket along one side of each chicken breast. Divide the filling into 4 portions and ease a portion into each pocket. Pull the chicken flesh together to encase the filling.

3. Wrap a slice of Parma ham around each chicken breast: lay the ham over the breast, then fold the ends under to enclose and help seal in the filling.

4. Place the chicken breasts in an ovenproof dish, cover with foil and cook in the oven for 35-40 minutes.

5. Meanwhile, make the sauce. Place the tomatoes in a large bowl, pour over enough boiling water to cover and leave for 1 minute. Lift from the bowl and remove the skins. Roughly chop the tomato flesh.

6. Peel and finely chop the shallots. Grate the orange rind, squeeze the juice and pour 30 ml (2 tbsp) into a large pan. Stir in the chopped tomatoes, garlic and seasoning, cover and place over a medium heat to sweat for a few minutes. Stir in the marmalade. Bring to the boil, then simmer for about 20 minutes, until the mixture is of a spooning consistency.

7. To serve, place the chicken breasts on warmed serving plates, spoon over the sauce and garnish with orange wedges and herbs. Serve with a mixed green salad.

TECHNIQUE

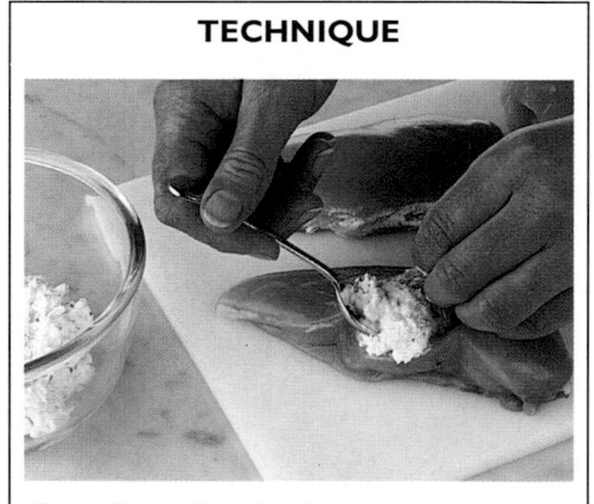

Cut a 5 cm (2 inch) slit along the thicker side of each chicken breast. Open up to form a pocket and fill with the ricotta mixture.

ROAST CHICKEN WITH PUMPKIN AND PEPPERS

Chicken should play a large part in a slim and healthy lifestyle – it's low in fat and high in protein. For extra flavour choose a free-range chicken. Roasting the chicken on a bed of pumpkins and peppers makes for an easy meal – the meat and vegetables are all cooked together. Use red and yellow peppers to contrast with the orange flesh of the pumpkin.

SERVES 4

1 yellow pepper
1 red pepper
575 g (1¼ lb) pumpkin or butternut squash
1 red onion
1 red chilli
1 lime
2 oranges
salt and pepper
1.5 kg (3 lb) free-range chicken
10 ml (2 tsp) jerk seasoning
300 ml (½ pint) chicken stock

PREPARATION TIME
20 minutes
COOKING TIME
1-1½ hours
FREEZING
Not suitable

345 CALS PER SERVING

1. Halve the peppers and remove the core and seeds. Cut the peppers into 2.5 cm (1 inch) chunks; set aside. Peel the pumpkin or squash with a sharp knife or vegetable peeler. Scoop out the seeds and stringy centre, then cut the pumpkin into wedges. Peel the onion and cut into wedges. Halve and deseed the chilli, then slice thinly. Spoon the prepared vegetables into the base of a roasting tin, leaving a space in the centre for the chicken.

2. Preheat the oven to 180°C (350°F) Mark 4. Thinly pare a few strips of lime and orange rind, cut into very thin strips and set aside. Grate the remaining rind and squeeze the juice. Pour the lime juice and 60 ml (4 tbsp) orange juice over the vegetables. Stir in the grated orange and lime rind and season with salt and pepper.

3. Place the chicken in the centre of the roasting tin amongst the vegetables. Brush with the remaining orange juice and rub in the jerk seasoning. Cook for 1-1½ hours, basting with the cooking juices about every 20 minutes.

4. Lift the chicken and vegetables onto a warmed serving platter. Strain off any fat, then pour the stock into the pan and bring to the boil. Add the reserved orange and lime strips and simmer for 10 minutes. Carve the chicken into thick slices and serve with the roasted vegetables, citrus gravy, and a seasonal green vegetable, if wished.

NOTE: If jerk seasoning is unobtainable, season the chicken with salt and paprika instead.

TECHNIQUE

Brush the chicken liberally all over with the mixed lime and orange juice.

CHICKEN SALAD WITH MARINATED CUCUMBER

A chicken salad is always a popular inclusion in a healthy diet. This one contains lots of fruit, salad leaves and vegetables. Vary the fruit if you wish – pears and grapes make good alternatives.

SERVES 4-6

4 skinless chicken breast fillets, each 125 g (4 oz)
1 small onion, peeled
1 small carrot, peeled
2 celery stalks
1 bay leaf
5 peppercorns
¼ small watermelon
1 green apple
5-10 ml (1-2 tsp) lemon juice
25 g (1 oz) pine nuts
25 g (1 oz) flaked almonds
MARINATED CUCUMBER
1 cucumber
175 ml (6 fl oz) white wine or tarragon vinegar
salt and pepper
HERB DRESSING
45 ml (3 tbsp) reduced-calorie mayonnaise
200 ml (7 fl oz) low-fat bio yogurt
1-2 spring onions, trimmed
45 ml (3 tbsp) chopped fresh mixed herbs, such as chives, parsley and tarragon
pinch of paprika
TO SERVE
50 g (2 oz) watercress
50 g (2 oz) rocket
50 g (2 oz) lamb's lettuce
25 g (1 oz) alfalfa sprouts
tarragon sprigs, to garnish

PREPARATION TIME 30 minutes
COOKING TIME 20 minutes
FREEZING Not suitable

375-255 CALS PER SERVING

1. Place the chicken breasts in a flameproof casserole or heavy-based pan. Pour on enough water just to cover, and add the peeled whole onion and carrot, celery, bay leaf and peppercorns. Bring to the boil, lower the heat, cover and poach gently for 20 minutes, or until cooked.

2. Meanwhile, prepare the cucumber. Peel the cucumber with a vegetable peeler, cut in half lengthways, then scoop out and discard the seeds with a teaspoon. Thinly slice the cucumber and place in a bowl. Sprinkle with the vinegar and seasoning and leave to marinate while the chicken is cooking.

3. Remove the cooked chicken from the poaching liquid and allow to cool.

4. Cut the watermelon into small wedges, discarding the skin and seeds. Cut the apple into quarters, remove the core and slice into 2.5 cm (1 inch) pieces. Brush with the lemon juice and set aside. Place the pine nuts and almonds on a baking sheet and toast under the grill for a few minutes until golden brown.

5. To make the herb dressing, mix the mayonnaise with the yogurt. Finely chop the spring onions. Stir into the yogurt mixture with the chopped herbs. Season with a little paprika.

6. Wash the salad leaves and arrange on a serving platter. Slice the cooked chicken into large strips and place on the leaves. Drain the marinated cucumber and add to the salad with the fruit. Scatter over the alfalfa sprouts and nuts, and drizzle over the dressing. Garnish with tarragon to serve.

VARIATION

Use another variety of melon, instead of watermelon, such as ogen or pink-fleshed Charentais.

TECHNIQUE

After peeling the cucumber and cutting in half lengthways, hold in one hand and scoop out the seeds with a teaspoon.

PAN-ROASTED PHEASANT IN A RED WINE AND THYME SAUCE

Game birds are a good alternative to chicken, as they have a similar nutritional content – low in fat, high in protein. Their strong gamey flavour makes them ideal for serving with a rich red wine sauce. Although only in season in the winter, pheasants are available frozen all year round. As an alternative, use guinea fowl.

SERVES 4

2 pheasants
30 ml (2 tbsp) plain flour
salt and pepper
1 small onion, peeled
4 fresh thyme sprigs
2 bay leaves
225 g (8 oz) chestnut mushrooms
15 ml (1 tbsp) olive oil
225 g (8 oz) small shallots, peeled
2 garlic cloves, crushed
150 ml (¼ pint) full-bodied red wine
15 ml (1 tbsp) each chopped fresh parsley and thyme
30 ml (2 tbsp) tomato purée
30 ml (2 tbsp) redcurrant jelly

TO GARNISH
rosemary sprigs

PREPARATION TIME
25 minutes
COOKING TIME
50 minutes
FREEZING
Not suitable

400 CALS PER SERVING

1. Remove any quills from the pheasants. Rinse the birds inside and out; pat dry. Using a sharp knife held close to the breast bone, cut along one side of the bone to remove the breast meat. Cut the leg joint from the body. Repeat on the other side, so you have 4 pieces from each bird. Remove the skin from the breasts and legs, then lightly coat the pieces in seasoned flour; set aside.

2. Place the carcasses in a large saucepan, cover with water and add the onion, thyme sprigs, seasoning and 1 bay leaf. Bring to the boil, cover and simmer for 30 minutes.

3. Wipe the mushrooms with a damp cloth; halve any large ones. Set aside.

4. Heat the oil in a flameproof casserole or heavy-based pan. Add the pheasant breasts and brown on both sides; remove and set aside. Add the leg pieces to the pan, brown on all sides, then remove and set aside.

5. Add the shallots and garlic to the pan and sauté until brown. Stir in the mushrooms and return the pheasant pieces to the pan. Pour on the red wine and bring to the boil to burn off the alcohol. Skim off the fat from the pheasant stock, then strain. Measure 350 ml (12 fl oz) and pour over the pheasant. Add the chopped herbs, bay leaf and tomato purée. Bring to the boil, cover and simmer gently for 20 minutes.

6. Transfer the pheasant pieces with a slotted spoon to a warmed serving plate and keep warm. Discard the bay leaf. Stir the redcurrant jelly into the stock, bring to the boil and boil for a few minutes to reduce and thicken. Pour over the pheasant, garnish with rosemary sprigs and serve with baby turnips and/or green vegetables.

TECHNIQUE

Cut the leg joints from the pheasants, using a very sharp knife.

MINTED LAMB ESCALOPES

Extra-lean, wafer-thin lamb escalopes are flavoured with a fresh-tasting minted yogurt marinade, then grilled to perfection. A colourful salad of baby spinach leaves, tomatoes and onion is the ideal accompaniment. Serve with some warm pitta bread, too.

SERVES 4

450 g (1 lb) lamb escalopes (see note)
MARINADE
90 ml (6 tbsp) Greek-style yogurt
1 garlic clove, crushed
60 ml (4 tbsp) chopped fresh mint
30 ml (2 tbsp) lemon juice
salt and coarsely ground black pepper
TO GARNISH
mint sprigs

PREPARATION TIME
10 minutes, plus marinating
COOKING TIME
6 minutes
FREEZING
Not suitable

210 CALS PER SERVING

1. For the marinade, mix the yogurt, crushed garlic, chopped mint and lemon juice together in a shallow non-metallic dish. Season with salt and pepper. Add the lamb escalopes and turn to coat evenly in the yogurt mixture. Cover the dish and leave to marinate in a cool place for 2-3 hours.

2. Preheat the grill to high. Place the lamb escalopes on the grill rack in a single layer. Grill for 3 minutes on each side or until golden brown and cooked through, basting occasionally with the marinade.

3. Transfer the lamb to warmed serving plates and garnish with mint sprigs. Serve with a spinach, tomato and onion salad, and warm pitta bread.

NOTE: For this recipe, you need very thin lean escalopes cut from the leg. These are sold ready-prepared in some supermarkets; alternatively ask your butcher to prepare them for you.

VARIATION

For spiced lamb escalopes, replace the mint with 5 ml (1 tsp) each ground cumin and turmeric, and 2.5 cm (1 inch) piece fresh root ginger, grated.

TECHNIQUE

Add the lamb escalopes to the minted yogurt marinade and turn to coat evenly.

ORIENTAL BEEF STIR-FRY

Stir-frying is a favourite Chinese cooking method. Here tender strips of beef are stir-fried in an oriental sauce of black and yellow bean sauce, which combines well with the rich earthy flavour of beef. Using lots of vegetables in your cooking increases the amount of fibre, vitamins and minerals in your diet.

SERVES 4-6

350 g (12 oz) fillet steak
2 bunches of spring onions
2 orange peppers
1 red chilli
225 g (8 oz) broccoli
175 g (6 oz) spinach (or pak choi or choi sam)
15 ml (1 tbsp) chilli or stir-fry oil

MARINADE

30 ml (2 tbsp) sherry vinegar
30 ml (2 tbsp) black bean sauce
30 ml (2 tbsp) yellow bean sauce
2.5 cm (1 inch) piece fresh root ginger
15 ml (1 tbsp) dark soy sauce

PREPARATION TIME
20 minutes, plus marinating beef
COOKING TIME
10-15 minutes
FREEZING
Not suitable

200-135 CALS PER SERVING

1. First, prepare the marinade. Mix the sherry vinegar with the black and yellow bean sauces. Peel and crush the ginger and add to the mixture with the soy sauce.

2. Slice the fillet steak into thin strips, about 5 cm (2 inches) long and 1 cm (½ inch) wide. Stir into the marinade. Cover and leave to marinate in a cool place for at least 30 minutes or up to 12 hours in the refrigerator.

3. Trim the spring onions and cut into diagonal strips about 5 cm (2 inches) long. Cut the peppers and chilli in half, remove and discard the seeds. Slice the peppers into thin strips; cut the chilli into very fine strips. Cut the broccoli into small even florets. Shred the spinach.

4. Drain the meat from the marinade, using a draining spoon. Heat the oil in a large non-stick frying pan or wok, add the meat and cook for 3-4 minutes, stirring. Stir in the vegetables and cook for 3-4 minutes. Stir in the marinade and heat through for 3-4 minutes. Serve immediately, with noodles.

NOTE: Stir-fried food is cooked in minutes in very little oil, so the natural flavours and textures are retained. Swirling the hot oil over the surface of the pan just before adding the food produces an even heat.

TECHNIQUE

Marinate the strips of fillet steak in the sherry vinegar, bean sauce, ginger and soy sauce mixture before stir-frying.

BASMATI VEGETABLE PILAF

A medley of steamed vegetables in a spicy basmati rice mixture. The rice provides both protein and carbohydrate, while the seeds add texture and increase the nutritional value (see note). The vegetables should be just tender, but still firm enough to add a crunchiness to the dish, as well as colour.

SERVES 4

1 small cauliflower
225 g (8 oz) baby carrots
2 courgettes
175 g (6 oz) patty pans
175 g (6 oz) okra
handful of baby spinach leaves (optional)
1 onion
15 ml (1 tbsp) sunflower oil
5 ml (1 tsp) green cardamom pods, seeds removed and crushed
5 ml (1 tsp) cumin seeds
5 ml (1 tsp) black mustard seeds (optional)
2 long cinnamon sticks
10 ml (2 tsp) garam masala
300 g (10 oz) brown basmati rice
300 ml (½ pint) vegetable stock
150 ml (¼ pint) apple juice
400 g (14 oz) can tomatoes
30 ml (2 tbsp) pumpkin seeds
CUCUMBER RAITA
⅓ cucumber
1 lime
30 ml (2 tbsp) chopped fresh mint
150 ml (¼ pint) low-fat bio yogurt
salt and pepper

PREPARATION TIME 20 minutes
COOKING TIME 25-30 minutes
FREEZING Not suitable

520 CALS PER SERVING

1. Break the cauliflower into small even-sized florets. Scrub the carrots and leave whole, trimming the root and leaving on a tuft of stalk. Cut the courgettes into 2.5 cm (1 inch) chunks. Cut the patty pans in half; trim the okra. Clean the spinach thoroughly, if using.

2. Peel the onion and cut into large chunks. Heat the oil in a non-stick pan, add the onion and fry gently until soft. Stir in the spices and cook for a few minutes to release the flavours.

3. Wash the basmati rice in a sieve under cold running water; drain well. Add to the pan, stirring well to coat with the oil and spices. Pour in the hot vegetable stock, add the apple juice and the tomatoes with their juice. Bring to the boil and simmer for 10 minutes.

4. Stir in the prepared vegetables, except the spinach. Cover and simmer gently for 15-20 minutes, until just tender but still firm. Add the spinach leaves, if using, and fold in until just wilted.

5. Meanwhile, prepare the raita. Grate the cucumber and place in a small dish. Finely grate the rind from the lime and squeeze the juice. Add to the cucumber with the chopped mint. Stir in the yogurt and season with salt and pepper.

6. Place the pumpkin seeds on a baking tray and toast under a preheated grill for a few minutes until golden. To serve, stir the pumpkin seeds into the pilaf and accompany with the raita.

NOTE: If you are following a vegetarian diet, seeds play a very beneficial part, providing useful amounts of the B vitamins. Pumpkin, sunflower, sesame and poppy seeds are readily available from most large supermarkets.

TECHNIQUE

Add the rice to the onion and spices, stirring well to coat.

SUMMER VEGETABLE RISOTTO

For this quick and easy vegetarian risotto, use whatever green vegetables are fresh and in season. Just make sure they are blanched until barely tender before stirring into the rice mixture.

SERVES 4

700 g (1½ lb) mixed French beans, broad beans, mangetouts, peas and asparagus
12 pitted black olives
350 g (12 oz) tomatoes
4 sun-dried tomatoes in oil, drained (optional)
225 g (8 oz) mixed wild and long-grain rice
350 ml (12 fl oz) vegetable stock
15 ml (1 tbsp) oil (from sun-dried tomatoes if using)
1 garlic clove, crushed
salt and pepper

PREPARATION TIME
5 minutes
COOKING TIME
About 25 minutes
FREEZING
Not suitable

350-375 CALS PER SERVING

1. Trim the green vegetables and blanch in boiling water until barely tender. Drain and refresh under cold running water; drain well. Halve the olives. Dice the fresh and sun-dried tomatoes if using.

2. Put the rice and stock in a saucepan. Bring to the boil, lower the heat and simmer, covered, for about 20 minutes or until all the liquid has been absorbed and the rice is tender.

3. Heat the oil in a large non-stick frying pan or wok. Add the garlic and cook, stirring, for 1-2 minutes.

4. Add the tomatoes and rice. Cook, stirring, over a gentle heat for 3-4 minutes. Stir in the blanched vegetables and olives. Increase the heat and cook, stirring, for 1 minute until piping hot. Season with salt and pepper to taste and serve immediately.

NOTE: Packets of mixed wild and long-grain rice are readily available from supermarkets. Refer to the packet instructions for the recommended cooking time. To test if rice is cooked, remove a few grains from the pan and press between finger and thumb. If it squashes easily and there is no hard core the rice is ready.

TECHNIQUE

Stir-fry the rice with the diced fresh and sun-dried tomatoes over a low heat for 3-4 minutes.

PET-ASPA
QUALITY

PASTA WITH ROASTED VEGETABLES

Pappardelle is a wide ribbon pasta which always looks attractive served with vegetables. Here it is tossed in a light, fresh-flavoured sauce and topped with roasted Mediterranean vegetables, to make a wonderful wholesome dish with an intense flavour.

SERVES 4

1 fennel bulb
2 yellow peppers
1 red onion
2 garlic cloves, peeled
15 ml (1 tbsp) olive oil
150 ml (¼ pint) low-fat bio yogurt
125 g (4 oz) ricotta or other curd cheese
30 ml (2 tbsp) semi-skimmed milk
30 ml (2 tbsp) chopped fresh basil
30 ml (2 tbsp) chopped fresh parsley
salt and pepper
350 g (12 oz) fresh pappardelle or tagliatelle
30 ml (2 tbsp) freshly grated Parmesan cheese
30 ml (2 tbsp) black olives
30 ml (2 tbsp) capers
TO GARNISH
flat-leaf parsley

PREPARATION TIME
20 minutes
COOKING TIME
20-25 minutes
FREEZING
Not suitable

485 CALS PER SERVING

1. Preheat the oven to 220°C (425°F) Mark 7. Trim the fennel and cut lengthwise into slices, about 2.5 cm (1 inch) thick; reserve a few fronds for garnish. Cut the peppers in half, remove the seeds and core and cut into broad 2.5 cm (1 inch) long strips. Peel and slice the onion. Place the vegetables, including the whole garlic cloves, on a baking sheet. Brush lightly with the oil and bake in the oven for 20-25 minutes, until browning along the edges.

2. Meanwhile, place the yogurt, cheese and milk in a bowl. Add the basil and parsley, season liberally with black pepper and mix to form a pale green sauce. Transfer the sauce to a pan and heat through gently.

3. Cook the pasta in a large pan of boiling salted water for 4-5 minutes, until *al dente* (tender but firm to the bite); drain thoroughly. Add to the sauce with the Parmesan and toss well. Transfer to a warmed serving dish.

4. Remove the vegetables from the oven, mix in the olives and capers and serve on top of the pasta. Garnish with flat-leaf parsley and the reserved fennel fronds. Serve at once.

VARIATION

For a roasted ratatouille sauce, replace the fennel with 1 small aubergine; a few tomatoes and 1-2 courgettes. Roast as above. Omit the capers.

TECHNIQUE

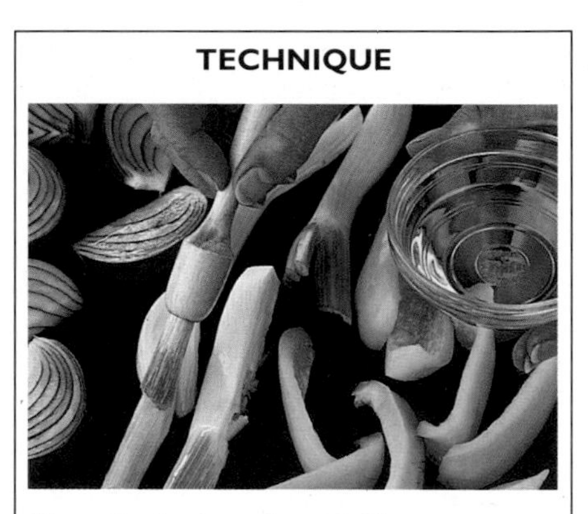

Place the prepared vegetables on a baking sheet and brush lightly with oil before roasting.

LENTIL, BEAN AND VEGETABLE GRATIN

A delicious mixture using the best pulses – Puy lentils and flageolet beans. Both have a good flavour and hold their shape well when cooked. Here Puy lentils are simmered in stock with red wine and herbs, then combined with canned flageolets. The addition of sweet potato makes a nutritious and tasty dish. A crunchy breadcrumb topping – flavoured with goat's cheese, herbs and tomatoes – is the perfect complement.

SERVES 4

1 onion
1 carrot
2 celery stalks
225 g (8 oz) sweet potato
15 ml (1 tbsp) sunflower oil
1 garlic clove, crushed
10 ml (2 tsp) sun-dried tomato paste or tomato purée
300 ml (½ pint) red wine
125 g (4 oz) Puy lentils
450 ml (¾ pint) vegetable stock
1 bay leaf
30 ml (2 tbsp) chopped fresh parsley
½ x 300 g (10 oz) can flageolet beans, drained and rinsed
salt and pepper

TOPPING

125 g (4 oz) goat's cheese
50 g (2 oz) wholemeal breadcrumbs
15 ml (1 tbsp) chopped fresh parsley
15 ml (1 tbsp) chopped fresh thyme
450 g (1 lb) plum tomatoes (or other flavourful tomatoes)

PREPARATION TIME 15 minutes
COOKING TIME 1-1¼ hours
FREEZING Suitable

410 CALS PER SERVING

1. Peel and finely chop the onion and carrot. Trim and finely chop the celery. Peel the sweet potato and cut into 2.5 cm (1 inch) chunks.

2. Heat the oil in a large pan, add the prepared vegetables and garlic and sauté for a few minutes to soften. Stir in the sun-dried tomato paste or tomato purée and wine. Bring to the boil and cook for 1 minute.

3. Wash the lentils under cold running water. Drain and add to the pan with the stock, bay leaf and parsley. Bring to the boil and simmer for 45 minutes to 1 hour or until the lentils are soft. Add the canned beans and heat through. Taste and adjust the seasoning. Discard the bay leaf.

4. Meanwhile, prepare the topping. Crumble the cheese and stir into the breadcrumbs with the parsley and thyme. Roughly chop the tomatoes.

5. Preheat the grill to medium. Spoon the bean and lentil mixture into an ovenproof gratin dish. Scatter the chopped tomatoes over the beans, then top with the breadcrumb mixture. Place under the grill for about 10 minutes, until the topping is just crisp. Serve with a watercress and spinach salad and crusty bread.

NOTE: Use the remaining flageolet beans as a vegetable accompaniment to a light main course: toss in a little balsamic vinegar and sprinkle with chopped parsley; or use in a mixed bean salad.

TECHNIQUE

To make the topping, mix the breadcrumbs with the goat's cheese and herbs.

FILO MUSHROOM TARTLETS

There is now a good selection of mushrooms available in most supermarkets. They are an ideal ingredient for vegetarian cooking as they have a good flavour and texture which combines well with many other ingredients. Here they are mixed with sun-dried tomatoes and used to fill crisp filo flan cases. Topped with an egg and then baked, these individual tarts make a stunning dish to serve as a light meal or substantial starter.

SERVES 6

8-10 sheets filo pastry
15 ml (1 tbsp) sunflower oil
FILLING
2 small red onions
15 ml (1 tbsp) sunflower oil
2 garlic cloves, crushed
125 g (4 oz) chestnut mushrooms
125 g (4 oz) flat mushrooms
5 sun-dried tomatoes in oil, drained
10 ml (2 tsp) lemon juice
15 ml (1 tbsp) chopped fresh parsley
salt and pepper
6 eggs (size 3)
15 g (½ oz) freshly grated Parmesan cheese
TO SERVE
mixed lettuce leaves
balsamic vinegar

PREPARATION TIME
30 minutes
COOKING TIME
25-30 minutes
FREEZING
Not suitable

375 CALS PER SERVING

1. Preheat the oven to 190°C (375°F) Mark 5. Lightly grease six 9 cm (3½ inch), 2.5 cm (1 inch) deep flan tins. Cut the filo pastry into eighteen 11 cm (4½ inch) squares. Brush each square with a little sunflower oil. Layer 3 sheets in each tin, arranging them at an angle to each other so the points form a star. Press the pastry into the sides of the tins. Bake for 10-15 minutes until just golden and crispy (don't overcook them as they have to be baked again).

2. Meanwhile, prepare the filling. Peel and finely chop the onions. Heat the oil in a pan, add the onions and fry until softened and transparent. Add the garlic. Wipe the mushrooms clean with a damp cloth, then chop finely. Add to the pan and cook until the juices start to run.

3. Chop the sun-dried tomatoes very finely. Stir into the cooked mushrooms with the lemon juice, parsley and seasoning.

4. Divide the filling between the prepared pastry cases. Make a well in the centre with the back of a spoon, pushing the filling to the side. Break one egg into a small saucer or small cup, then slide into the well in a tart. Repeat with the remainder. Sprinkle with the Parmesan cheese. Return to the oven and cook for 14-16 minutes until the eggs are softly set and creamy, depending on how you prefer them cooked. Serve with a mixed leaf salad drizzled with balsamic vinegar.

TECHNIQUE

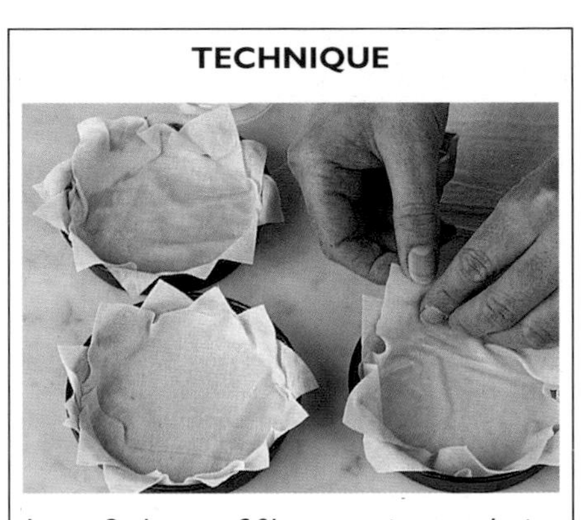

Layer 3 sheets of filo pastry into each tin, overlapping the pastry to form a star shape.

SPINACH AND FETA CHEESE PIZZA

Because you're following a healthy diet doesn't mean you have to cut out some of your favourite foods. Pizzas are not all bad, as long as you avoid those topped with lots of cheese, which is high in fat. By making your own you can decide on the topping and pack it full of vegetables.

SERVES 6

PIZZA DOUGH

125 g (4 oz) strong plain white flour
125 g (4 oz) wholemeal flour
50 g (2 oz) semolina
pinch of salt
15 g (½ oz) butter or margarine, in pieces
15 ml (1 tbsp) finely chopped fresh rosemary
0.5 g (½ oz) easy-blend fast-action dried yeast

TOPPING

450 g (1 lb) baby spinach leaves
2 courgettes
3 tomatoes
30 ml (2 tbsp) sun-dried tomato paste
125 g (4 oz) feta or goat's cheese
2 garlic cloves, crushed
pepper
12 black olives
15 ml (1 tbsp) olive oil

PREPARATION TIME
30 minutes
COOKING TIME
15-20 minutes
FREEZING Not suitable

295 CALS PER SERVING

1. First, make the pizza dough. Place the plain and wholemeal flours, semolina and salt in a bowl and mix together well. Rub in the butter or margarine. Add the rosemary and yeast and stir in about 200 ml (7 fl oz) warm water, just enough to form a soft dough. Knead lightly until smooth, place in a large bowl, cover with a tea-towel and leave to rise in a warm place for 45 minutes.

2. Meanwhile, prepare the topping. Clean the spinach thoroughly. Shred finely and cook in a covered pan, with just the water that clings to the leaves after washing, for 3 minutes or until wilted. Refresh under cold water to retain the colour. Dry well and squeeze out excess moisture. Slice the courgettes diagonally. Slice the tomatoes.

3. Preheat the oven to 220°C (425°F) Mark 7. Roll out the pizza dough into one large 30 cm (12 inch) circle or two 20 cm (8 inch) circles and lay on greased baking sheets. Spread with the sun-dried tomato paste. Scatter the cooked spinach over the pizza base(s). Cover with the courgette slices, then top with the tomato slices.

4. Crumble the feta or goat's cheese over the vegetables and sprinkle with the garlic. Grind over some black pepper, scatter with the olives and drizzle over a little olive oil.

5. Bake in the oven for 15-20 minutes, until well risen. Using a fish slice, lift the pizza(s) onto a wire rack and leave to cool for a few minutes. Serve with a crisp green salad.

VARIATION

Vary the vegetables according to taste and availability. Try thinly sliced button mushrooms, sliced peppers and canned artichoke hearts.

TECHNIQUE

Arrange the courgette slices on the pizza base, covering the spinach.

ROASTED SQUASH AND PEPPER BAKE

This is a really colourful bake, ideal for serving to vegetarians. Squash has a wonderful sweetness and dense texture which makes it a good base for a bake. Yellow and red peppers add colour and flavour. The tomato sauce has a touch of spiciness balanced with a little marmalade for sweetness.

SERVES 4

2 butternut squash, about 1 kg (2 lb) total weight
30 ml (2 tbsp) orange juice
30 ml (2 tbsp) chopped fresh coriander
1 red onion
1 yellow pepper
1 red pepper
25 g (1 oz) freshly grated Parmesan cheese
25 g (1 oz) pine nuts
TOMATO SAUCE
450 g (1 lb) tomatoes
2 shallots
1 red chilli
30 ml (2 tbsp) olive oil
2 garlic cloves, crushed
15 ml (1 tbsp) orange marmalade
pinch of paprika
salt and pepper

PREPARATION TIME
20 minutes
COOKING TIME
45-55 minutes
FREEZING
Not suitable

300 CALS PER SERVING

1. First, prepare the tomato sauce. Immerse the tomatoes in a large bowl of boiling water for 1 minute. Drain and refresh under cold running water, then peel away the skins. Roughly chop the flesh. Peel and finely chop the shallots. Halve, deseed and finely chop the chilli. (Wear rubber gloves to do this to avoid skin irritation.)

2. Heat the olive oil in a large pan. Stir in the shallots, garlic and chilli and fry gently for a few minutes until soft. Stir in the prepared tomatoes, add the marmalade, and season with paprika, salt and pepper to taste. Cover and simmer for 20 minutes.

3. Meanwhile, preheat the oven to 200°C (400°F) Mark 6 and prepare the squash. Cut in half, scoop out the seeds and discard. Remove the skin with a sharp knife or vegetable peeler and cut the flesh into small pieces; the skin is quite tough, so you may find it easier to cut the squash into small pieces first and then remove the skin. Place in a large ovenproof dish. Add the orange juice and coriander; toss well.

4. Peel and slice the onion into strips. Cut the peppers in half, remove the core and seeds, then cut into small cubes. Add to the squash and season with salt and pepper. Spoon over the hot tomato sauce, then sprinkle with the Parmesan and pine nuts. Bake in the oven for 45-55 minutes until the top is golden.

5. Serve immediately, as a vegetable accompaniment with roast lamb, or with a green vegetable as a vegetarian main course.

VARIATION

Replace the squash with sweet potatoes. For speed, instead of making a tomato sauce slice the tomatoes, chop the shallots and crush the garlic and arrange in the dish in layers with the squash and peppers. Mix the olive oil with 60 ml (4 tbsp) pesto sauce and pour over the top. Bake as above.

TECHNIQUE

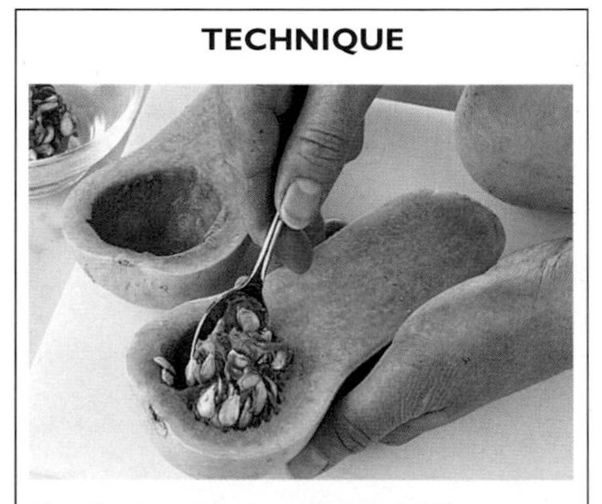

Cut the butternut squash in half, scoop out and discard the seeds.

POTATO AND LEEK PARCELS WITH GARLIC AND ROSEMARY

Potatoes are probably the most versatile ingredient available. Not only are there many varieties, but also many different ways of cooking them, from a creamy, comforting mash, to the first-of-the-season Jersey royal new potatoes, cooked in their skins and served with unsalted butter. In this recipe they are steamed with leeks in a paper parcel. Use either new potatoes or older larger ones, cut into even-sized pieces.

SERVES 4-6

225 g (8 oz) leeks
450 g (1 lb) potatoes
3 garlic cloves, unpeeled
4 fresh rosemary sprigs
sea salt and pepper
30 ml (2 tbsp) olive oil

PREPARATION TIME
10 minutes
COOKING TIME
1 hour
FREEZING
Not suitable

165-110 CALS PER SERVING

1. Preheat the oven to 200°C (400°F) Mark 6. Trim the leeks, clean thoroughly and cut into 2.5 cm (1 inch) thick slices. Scrub the potatoes thoroughly. If using large potatoes, cut into small even-sized pieces and dry thoroughly.

2. Place a large sheet of greaseproof paper in a roasting tin, so that it covers the base and sides. Arrange the potatoes and leeks in the pan, add the garlic and rosemary, season with salt and pepper and pour over the oil.

3. Take another sheet of greaseproof paper and lay over the top to cover completely. Fold the edges of both sheets together to seal. Bake in the oven for 1 hour until tender; for crisp potatoes, remove the top sheet of paper for the last 20 minutes of cooking.

4. To serve, remove from the greaseproof paper package and place in a warmed serving dish. Serve with roasted meat or fish, such as Monkfish with Pesto (page 26).

VARIATIONS

Other root vegetables, such as small carrots, turnips and parsnips, can be cooked in this way.

NOTE: Olive oil is ideal to use for salad dressings and cooking. Not only does it impart a good flavour, but also contains polyunsaturated fats, which are better for you. There is a vast selection of olive oils available, in different grades and flavours. Extra-virgin olive oil is the top grade and is good for salads or poured over warm vegetables. Use plain olive oil for cooking. The flavour varies according to the country and region of origin, so experiment with different ones.

TECHNIQUE

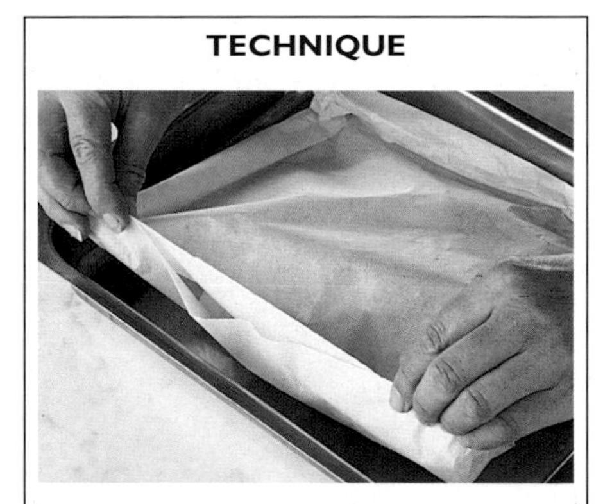

Cover the potatoes and leeks with a second sheet of greaseproof paper. Fold the edges of both sheets together to seal.

ROASTED PEPPERS WITH ORIENTAL DRESSING

This simple colourful salad is an ideal accompaniment to cold chicken and turkey. It's also delicious served warm: simply reheat the peppers under the grill for 3-4 minutes and warm the dressing in a pan for 2-3 minutes. Serve with grilled or roast meats.

SERVES 4

2 red peppers
1 yellow pepper
1 orange pepper
DRESSING
½ small red chilli
½ small green chilli
15 g (½ oz) piece fresh root ginger
1 small bunch of spring onions
60 ml (4 tbsp) soy sauce
60 ml (4 tbsp) lemon juice
15 ml (1 tbsp) white wine vinegar
30 ml (2 tbsp) clear honey

PREPARATION TIME
10 minutes
COOKING TIME
10-15 minutes
FREEZING
Not suitable

70 CALS PER SERVING

1. Preheat the grill to hot. Cut the peppers in half. Place cut-side down on the grill rack and grill for 10-15 minutes or until the skins become blackened and blistered all over. Cover with a clean damp tea-towel and leave to cool.

2. To prepare the dressing, halve, deseed and finely chop the chillis. (Wear rubber gloves to do this to avoid skin irritation.) Peel and finely shred or chop the ginger. Trim and slice the spring onions diagonally.

3. Place all the dressing ingredients in a small bowl and whisk together until thoroughly combined.

4. Remove the skin and seeds from the charred peppers, then cut into thick slices. Spoon the dressing over the peppers to serve.

VARIATION

For a 'less hot' version, omit the red and green chillies from the dressing. Sprinkle a little chopped coriander or parsley over the peppers to serve.

TECHNIQUE

Cover the grilled pepper halves with a clean damp tea-towel and leave to cool. The steam helps to lift the skins.

MIXED LEAF SALAD WITH CROÛTONS

A crisp, colourful salad featuring peppery rocket, watercress and radishes. Crunchy grilled croûtons are the perfect complement – heart-shaped ones look particularly attractive, but you can of course use any cutter or simply cut the bread into squares. Vary the salad leaves according to availability.

SERVES 6-8

1 head of radicchio
1 bunch of watercress
½ head of fine frisée
50 g (2 oz) baby spinach leaves
50 g (2 oz) rocket
250 g (9 oz) radishes
5 thin slices of bread
FRENCH DRESSING
30 ml (2 tbsp) olive oil
30 ml (2 tbsp) vegetable oil
22 ml (1½ tsp) white wine vinegar
pinch of sugar
1 small garlic clove, crushed
salt and pepper

PREPARATION TIME
10 minutes
COOKING TIME
3-4 minutes
FREEZING
Not suitable

140 CALS PER SERVING

1. Tear the radicchio into bite-sized pieces; cut the stalks off the watercress; discard any tough outer leaves from the frisée. Wash all the salad leaves in cold water. Drain and pat dry. Halve or quarter the radishes. Put the salad leaves and radishes in a large polythene bag and refrigerate until needed.

2. Preheat the grill. Using a heart-shaped cutter, stamp out shapes from the bread. Grill until golden on both sides.

3. For the French dressing, put all the ingredients in a screw-topped jar and shake vigorously to combine.

4. To serve, transfer the salad leaves and radishes to a serving bowl. Pour on the dressing and toss lightly. Scatter the warm croûtons over the salad and serve at once.

NOTE: French dressing is a hidden source of calories. Just 15 ml (1 tbsp) contains 105 calories. Slimmers may prefer to use a low-calorie version.

VARIATION

Replace the rocket with lamb's lettuce (mâche). Use oakleaf lettuce instead of the frisée.

TECHNIQUE

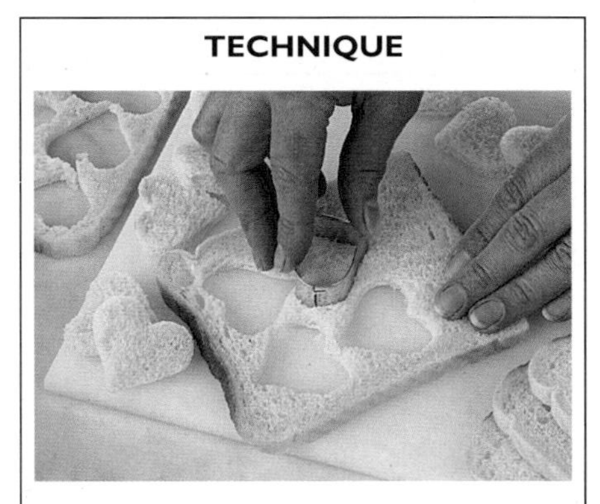

For the croûtons, use a heart-shaped cutter to stamp out hearts from the bread.

CHICORY, CELERY AND FLAGEOLET BEAN SALAD

A crisp crunchy salad of winter leaves – featuring long-leafed chicory, which has a slightly bitter flavour, red radicchio to add a burst of colour and crunchy celery. These are then tossed with green flageolet or white cannellini beans in a garlic-infused caper and anchovy dressing.

SERVES 4-6

1 head of celery
4 chicory bulbs
1 head of radicchio
50 g (2 oz) can anchovy fillets
½ x 300 g (10 oz) can flageolet or cannellini beans
30 ml (2 tbsp) chopped fresh parsley
DRESSING
45 ml (3 tbsp) olive oil
1 garlic clove, peeled
45 ml (3 tbsp) white wine vinegar
25 g (1 oz) capers
pepper
TO GARNISH
flat-leaf parsley sprigs

PREPARATION TIME
30 minutes
FREEZING
Not suitable

182-125 CALS PER SERVING

1. Trim and discard the base of the celery, trim and reserve the top, then cut into 1 cm (½ inch) diagonal slices; include the heart and the leaves, as these add a good flavour.

2. Break the chicory into individual leaves; this may be easier to do under cold running water, as the leaves will come away from the heart more easily. Remove the hard core from the radicchio and slice the leaves into strips. Mix the salad leaves together in a bowl.

3. To prepare the dressing, pour the olive oil into a pan, add the garlic and heat through gently until golden. Remove from the heat, discard the garlic, then add the vinegar, capers and pepper to the oil. Leave to infuse for a few minutes.

4. Drain the anchovies, stretch them with the back of a knife and cut into thin strips. Drain and rinse the beans and add to the salad leaves with the anchovy fillets and chopped parsley. Pour over the dressing and garnish with parsley sprigs to serve.

NOTE: Use the remaining canned beans to make a salad. Combine with other canned beans in an olive oil, balsamic vinegar and chopped fresh herb dressing.

VARIATION

During the summer, use tender young broad beans instead of flageolet or cannellini beans. Blanch in boiling water for 1 minute, then slip off the skins.

TECHNIQUE

Divide the chicory bulbs into individual leaves under cold running water.

FENNEL, POTATO AND ROCKET SALAD

Roasted fennel tossed in a light refreshing lemon dressing with baby new potatoes and rocket leaves makes a delicious vegetable accompaniment. Fennel is a popular ingredient in Italian cooking – it has a lovely crunchy texture and very slight aniseed flavour. Roasting softens both the texture and flavour. Serve with chicken, veal or pork dishes, or as a starter for 4.

SERVES 4-6

2 heads of fennel
15 ml (1 tbsp) olive oil
sea salt
2 garlic cloves, crushed
225 g (8 oz) new potatoes
175 g (6 oz) rocket leaves
225 g (8 oz) cherry tomatoes
DRESSING
1 lemon
10 ml (2 tsp) wholegrain mustard
25 ml (1 fl oz) olive oil
salt and pepper
TO GARNISH
25 g (1 oz) fresh Parmesan cheese

PREPARATION TIME
20 minutes
COOKING TIME
20 minutes
FREEZING
Not suitable

150-105 CALS PER SERVING

1. Preheat the oven to 230°C (450°F) mark 8. Trim the fennel, removing the base. Cut in half lengthwise and place in a roasting tin. Brush with olive oil and sprinkle with a little sea salt and the garlic. Cook in the oven for about 20 minutes, turning occasionally, until golden brown and softened. Remove from the oven and set aside.

2. Scrub the new potatoes thoroughly, then cook in boiling salted water for 15 minutes or until just tender. Drain thoroughly.

3. Wash and dry the rocket, discarding any bruised leaves. Place in a salad bowl. Cut the roasted fennel into pieces and add to the bowl. Cut the tomatoes in half and add to the bowl with the potatoes. Toss together lightly.

4. To make the dressing, grate the rind from the lemon and squeeze the juice into a bowl. Stir in the mustard and lemon rind, whisk in the olive oil and season with salt and pepper. Pour over the salad. Sprinkle with shavings of Parmesan and serve at once.

VARIATION

Replace the potato with pasta shapes, such as twists, shells or tubes. Cook in boiling salted water until tender, rinse under cold running water and drain well. Add to the salad with the tomatoes.

For an elegant starter, arrange the rocket leaves on individual serving plates and place the roasted fennel in the centre. Slice the potatoes and arrange around the fennel with curls of fresh Parma ham. Finish with wafer-thin slices of Parmesan cheese. Pour the lemon dressing over the salad to serve.

TECHNIQUE

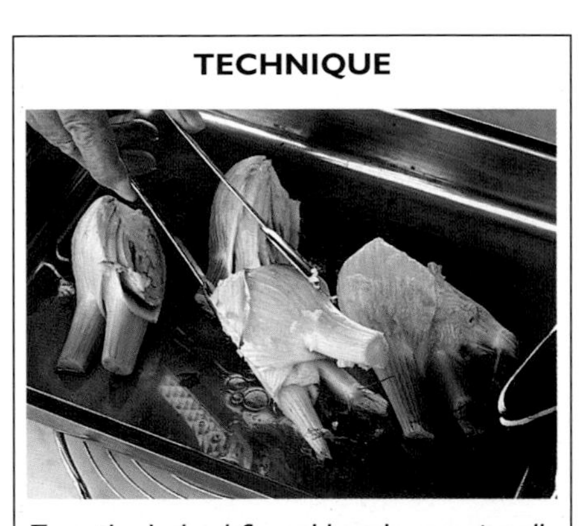

Turn the halved fennel heads occasionally during roasting to ensure they become golden brown all over.

FRAGRANT FRUIT SALAD

A fresh fruit salad is always a perfect end to a meal, especially a healthy one. This combination of fruit is pleasing both to the eye and palate, and can be varied according to taste and availability. If you feel you must serve something with it, try crème fraîche or fromage frais as a healthier alternative to cream.

SERVES 6

50 g (2 oz) caster sugar
grated rind and juice of 1 lemon
2 pieces of preserved stem ginger in syrup
60 ml (4 tbsp) ginger wine
700 g (1½ lb) lychees
3 ripe mangoes
450 g (1 lb) fresh or canned pineapple in natural juice
4 kiwi fruit
50 g (2 oz) Cape gooseberries, to decorate (optional)

PREPARATION TIME
20-30 minutes, plus chilling
COOKING TIME
Nil
FREEZING
Not suitable

175 CALS PER SERVING

1. Put the sugar in a pan with 150 ml (¼ pint) water and the lemon rind and juice. Heat gently until the sugar dissolves, then bring to the boil and simmer for 1 minute. Remove from the heat.

2. Finely chop the ginger and stir into the sugar syrup with the wine. Leave to cool while preparing the fruit.

3. Peel the lychees, cut in half and remove the shiny stones. Peel the mangoes and cut the flesh away from the stones. Cut the flesh into cubes.

4. If using fresh pineapple, peel, slice and remove the tough centre core from each slice. If using canned pineapple, drain well. Cut the pineapple slices into cubes. Peel and thinly slice the kiwi fruit. Cut the slices in half.

5. Place the fruit in a serving dish, pour over the syrup and toss lightly to mix. Cover with cling film and chill for several hours to allow the flavours to develop.

6. To decorate, peel back the calyx from each Cape gooseberry to form a 'flower'. Wipe the orange berry with a damp cloth. Arrange on top of the fruit salad to serve.

VARIATION

Replace one mango with 1-2 oranges, according to size. Pare the rind thinly and set aside. Remove the pith and segment the fruit. Cut the rind into very thin strips, blanch in boiling water for 1 minute and use to decorate the fruit salad if wished, in place of the Cape gooseberries.

TECHNIQUE

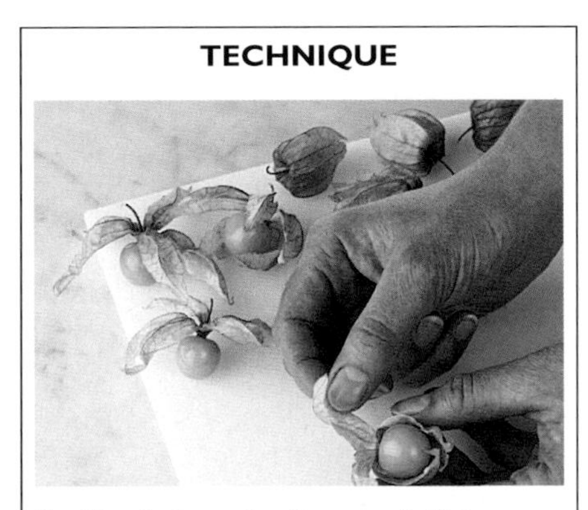

Peel back the calyx from each Cape gooseberry to form a 'flower'.

HOT MANGO AND BANANA SALAD

This is a fruit salad with a difference: it's served hot! The delicious combination of tropical tastes, spiked with a little rum, won't ruin your diet – as it provides less than 200 calories per portion. Quick to prepare, it makes an ideal midweek dessert that's something of a treat.

SERVES 4

- **2 large oranges**
- **2 firm but ripe mangoes, about 700 g (1 ½ lb) total weight**
- **4 small bananas**
- **25 g (1 oz) very low-fat spread**
- **5 ml (1 tsp) light soft brown sugar**
- **30 ml (2 tbsp) Malibu or rum**
- **30 ml (2 tbsp) lemon or lime juice**

PREPARATION TIME
10 minutes
COOKING TIME
5 minutes
FREEZING
Not suitable

200 CALS PER SERVING

1. Thinly pare the rind from one orange and squeeze the juice. Cut the pared rind into very thin strips and blanch in boiling water for 1 minute, to soften. Set the rind and juice aside. Peel the other orange with a serrated knife and slice the flesh crosswise into rounds.

2. Peel the mangoes with a vegetable peeler. Slice the flesh either side of the central stone, then remove any flesh from around the stone. Cut all the flesh into bite-sized pieces. Peel and thickly slice the bananas.

3. Melt the low-fat spread in a large non-stick frying pan. Add the sugar, mango and banana and sauté for 2-3 minutes or until just beginning to soften.

4. Pour in the Malibu or rum, lemon or lime juice and reserved orange juice. Add the orange slices. Bring to the boil, then serve immediately, decorated with the reserved orange rind.

NOTE: Mangoes are ripe when they yield to gentle pressure in your hand.

VARIATION

Guavas and pineapple also combine well with banana and mango and could be used instead of the orange slices, or in addition to make a larger salad. If you like a hint of spice, add 2.5 ml (1 tsp) ground cinnamon.

TECHNIQUE

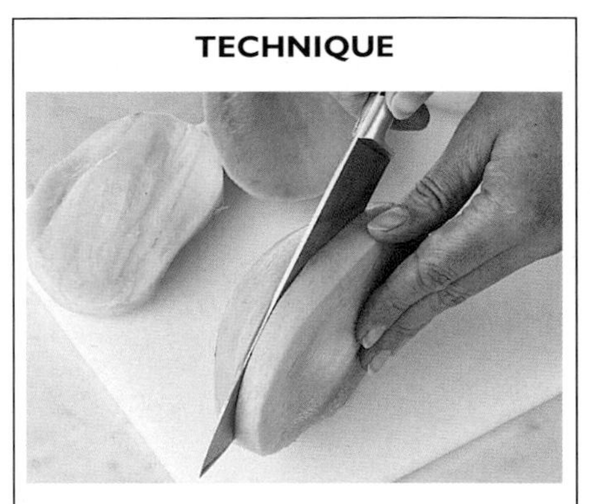

Slice the mango flesh either side of the central stone.

RED FRUIT TERRINE

An unusual way to serve the best of summer's soft fruits. Redcurrants, strawberries and raspberries are layered in a loaf tin to make an attractive fruit terrine. A special dinner party dessert that will be good for your guests – low in fat and high in fibre.

SERVES 6

65 g (2½ oz) caster sugar
275 ml (9 fl oz) medium-dry white wine
45 ml (3 tbsp) lemon juice
20 ml (4 tsp) powdered gelatine
225 g (8 oz) redcurrants
225 g (8 oz) medium ripe strawberries
225 g (8 oz) raspberries
TO DECORATE
mint sprigs
few strawberry slices
small redcurrant sprigs

PREPARATION TIME
55 minutes, plus chilling
COOKING TIME
Nil
FREEZING
Not suitable

100 CALS PER SERVING

1. Put the sugar in a pan with 250 ml (9 fl oz) water. Heat gently until the sugar dissolves, then bring to the boil and simmer for 1 minute. Pour into a bowl, cool, then stir in the wine and lemon juice.

2. Spoon 60 ml (4 tbsp) water into a small bowl and sprinkle over the gelatine. Soak for about 10 minutes or until sponge-like. Stand the bowl over a pan of gently simmering water for 2-3 minutes until it clears and liquefies. Pour into the wine syrup and leave to cool.

3. Strip the redcurrants off their stalks. Hull the strawberries, then slice into 5 mm (¼ inch) thick pieces.

4. Place a 1.1 litre (2 pint) non-stick loaf tin in a roasting pan. Surround the loaf tin with ice cubes and pour in enough cold water to come halfway up the sides of the tin. Arrange a thin layer of redcurrants over the base of the tin and gently spoon over enough liquid jelly to cover. Leave to set.

5. Cover with sliced strawberries, then a layer of raspberries. Repeat the layers, then carefully spoon over the remaining jelly to fill.

6. Leave the mould in the roasting pan until the jelly is just set, then transfer to the refrigerator for at least 3 hours or preferably overnight, to set completely.

7. To serve, fill a large bowl with hot water. Dip the loaf tin in the water for 3-4 seconds, then immediately invert onto a flat platter, gently shaking the tin to release the jelly. Decorate with mint sprigs, strawberry slices and redcurrants. Slice and serve with single cream or yogurt.

TECHNIQUE

Arrange the fruit in layers in the tin, then spoon over the jelly to fill.

INDIVIDUAL SUMMER PUDDINGS

An old favourite, individual summer puddings are ideal to serve as part of a healthy diet, especially if you use wholemeal bread. Fruit of any description is good to use as part of a healthy diet – full of vitamins, fruit sugars and fibre, but with very little fat. Summer puddings can be made into autumn puddings by using apples, pears and plums (see variation).

SERVES 6

10-12 large slices of wholemeal bread
300 g (10 oz) blackberries
400 g (14 oz) raspberries
125 g (4 oz) gooseberries
175 g (6 oz) redcurrants
150 ml (¼ pint) red grape juice
30 ml (2 tbsp) chopped mint
artificial sweetener or sugar, to taste
lemon balm or apple mint sprigs, to decorate

PREPARATION TIME
30 minutes
COOKING TIME
10-12 minutes
FREEZING
Suitable

160 CALS PER SERVING

1. Line six 150 ml (¼ pint) dariole moulds or individual pudding basins with cling film. Remove the crusts from the bread. Cut a 5 cm (2 inch) circle of bread to fit the base of each mould. Cut six 7.5 cm (3 inch) circles of bread and set aside. Cut the remaining bread into strips and use to line the sides of the moulds completely.

2. Hull the blackberries and raspberries, and top and tail the gooseberries. Strip the redcurrants off their stalks. Place the gooseberries in a saucepan with the grape juice, cover and cook for 5 minutes. Add the remaining fruit and cook gently until the currants start to burst and the juice runs; this will take 5-7 minutes. Stir the mint into the fruit and add artificial sweetener or sugar to taste.

3. While the fruit is still warm, spoon into the lined moulds, using a slotted spoon, and pour on sufficient fruit juice to moisten. Reserve the rest of the fruit juice. Cover with the reserved bread rounds. Top with a saucer or plate and press down with a heavy weight. Place in the refrigerator for several hours or overnight.

4. Turn out the puddings onto serving plates and pour on the reserved juice to cover them. Decorate with lemon balm or apple mint sprigs.

VARIATION

For an autumnal pudding, use cox's apples, pears and plums. Slice the fruit, removing the stones, cores and peel as necessary. Gently poach with apple mint for 10-15 minutes, until tender.

TECHNIQUE

Fill the lined moulds with the warm fruit, using a slotted spoon.

FROZEN VANILLA YOGURT WITH STRAWBERRY SAUCE

This is a delicious light frozen yogurt. Made with sheep's milk yogurt which is low in fat, it has a mild tangy flavour that combines well with the strawberry and balsamic vinegar sauce. If you wish to serve this during the winter, accompany with cinnamon-flavoured poached apples instead of strawberry sauce.

SERVES 6

FROZEN YOGURT
150 ml (¼ pint) semi-skimmed milk
5 ml (1 tsp) powdered gelatine
750 ml (1¼ pints) sheep's milk Greek yogurt
125 g (4 oz) Greek or wild flower-scented honey
2 egg whites
5 ml (1 tsp) vanilla essence
SAUCE
350 g (12 oz) strawberries
5-10 ml (1-2 tsp) balsamic vinegar
TO SERVE
225 g (8 oz) blueberries
lavender flowers, to decorate (optional)

PREPARATION TIME
35 minutes
COOKING TIME
Nil
FREEZING Suitable

235 CALS PER SERVING

1. Set the freezer to fast-freeze. Warm the milk in a saucepan until hot but not boiling. Remove from the heat and sprinkle over the gelatine, stirring quickly until it dissolves. Let cool slightly.

2. Mix the yogurt and honey together. When the gelatine has cooled to the same temperature as the yogurt, mix the two together.

3. Whisk the egg whites in a bowl until they form soft peaks, then fold into the yogurt mixture with a metal spoon. Stir in the vanilla essence. Freeze in an ice cream machine, according to manufacturer's instructions. Alternatively, turn into a freezerproof container, cover and freeze for 1½-2 hours, until beginning to freeze around the edge. Remove from the freezer, beat well or work in a food processor for a few seconds. Return to the freezer. Repeat twice more at 30 minute intervals, then freeze until firm.

4. To prepare the sauce, purée the strawberries in a blender or food processor. If preferred, pass the purée through a nylon sieve. Stir the balsamic vinegar into the strawberry purée and pour into a jug.

5. Remove the ice cream from the freezer 20-30 minutes before required, to soften. Scoop into chilled glasses, pour on the strawberry sauce and top with blueberries. Decorate with lavender flowers if wished.

VARIATION

Fold the strawberry purée into the half-frozen yogurt, after the final beating. Use other puréed fruits to flavour the ice cream. Spoon the half-frozen yogurt into individual ramekin dishes, after the final beating.

TECHNIQUE

Fold the whisked egg whites into the yogurt mixture with a metal spoon.

INDEX

If you would like further information about the **Good Housekeeping Cookery Club**, please write to:
Penny Smith, Ebury Press, Random House, 20 Vauxhall Bridge Road, London SW1V 2SA.